LANGUAGE IS POLITICS

Language is Politics discusses power relations between languages in the world, with a particular focus on English. Even though English is the most widely spoken and the most powerful language worldwide, it is not the lingua franca it is often supposed to be. The basic tenet of this book is that languages do not exist in the natural world; they are artefacts made by humans.

The book debunks some common myths about language and it suggests that we should be more modest in our assumptions, for instance concerning the linguistic uniqueness of our own species. The author argues in favour of an ecological or balanced approach to language. This approach sees humans and other animals as part of the larger ecosystems that life depends on. As in nature, diversity is crucial to the survival of languages. The current linguistic ecosystem is out of balance, and this book shows that education can help to restore the balance and cope with the challenges of a multilingual and multicultural world.

With an ecological approach to language and a focus on narratives and personal language histories, this will be key reading for researchers and academics, as well as students of English language and linguistics.

Frank van Splunder teaches academic writing in a multilingual context at Linguapolis, the language centre of the University of Antwerp. He holds a PhD in Applied Linguistics from Lancaster University.

He is a sociolinguist with a particular interest in relations between languages and how they are used to construct identities of people and nations. The focus of his research is English as the language of globalization and its use in higher education in non-English-speaking countries.

LANGUAGE IS POLITICS

Exploring an Ecological Approach to Language

Frank van Splunder

LONDON AND NEW YORK

First published 2020
by Routledge
2 Park Square, Milton Park, Abingdon, Oxon OX14 4RN

and by Routledge
52 Vanderbilt Avenue, New York, NY 10017

Routledge is an imprint of the Taylor & Francis Group, an informa business

© 2020 Frank van Splunder

The right of Frank van Splunder to be identified as author of this work has been asserted by him in accordance with Sections 77 and 78 of the Copyright, Designs and Patents Act 1988.

All rights reserved. No part of this book may be reprinted or reproduced or utilised in any form or by any electronic, mechanical, or other means, now known or hereafter invented, including photocopying and recording, or in any information storage or retrieval system, without permission in writing from the publishers.

Trademark notice: Product or corporate names may be trademarks or registered trademarks, and are used only for identification and explanation without intent to infringe.

British Library Cataloguing-in-Publication Data
A catalogue record for this book is available from the British Library

Library of Congress Cataloging-in-Publication Data
Names: Splunder, Frank van, author.
Title: Language is politics : exploring an ecological approach to language / Frank van Splunder.
Description: London ; New York : Routledge, 2020. | Includes bibliographical references and index.
Identifiers: LCCN 2019036227 | ISBN 9780367365431 (hardback) | ISBN 9780367365424 (paperback) | ISBN 9780429346880 (ebook)
Subjects: LCSH: Sociolinguistics. | Language–Political aspects. | Identity (Psychology) | Language and culture.
Classification: LCC P40 .S5966 2020 | DDC 306.44–dc23
LC record available at https://lccn.loc.gov/2019036227

ISBN: 978-0-367-36543-1 (hbk)
ISBN: 978-0-367-36542-4 (pbk)
ISBN: 978-0-429-34688-0 (ebk)

Typeset in Bembo
by Swales & Willis, Exeter, Devon, UK

Visit the eResources: www.routledge.com/9780367365424

CONTENTS

List of illustrations   *viii*
Acknowledgements   *ix*

Part 1
Language is politics   **1**

1. The language myth   **3**
   The invention of a myth   3
   The politics of language   7

2. The origin of language   **13**
   Colourless green ideas   13
   Natural and artificial languages   17
   Animal talk   21

3. Imagined communities   **25**
   Language and identity   25
   Language ideologies   27
   Imagining new communities   31

4. Language as a construction   **36**
   A dialect with an army   36
   Naming and shaming   38
   Constructing languages   40

5. The pecking order of languages — 48
World languages and other languages 48
The top ten of languages 52
Language and power 61

6. The power of English — 67
English as a world language 67
The rise of English 71
English in business, politics, and education 72

7. Language and war — 79
The war of words 79
The killing fields of language 84
The tsunami of English 88

8. Life and death of languages — 92
The struggle for life 92
Language birth 93
Language death 95

9. Towards an ecological approach to language — 101
Language and politics 101
Language and ecology 105

Part 2
Personal language histories — 111

1. Aim and scope 111
2. Asia 113
    Ifugao, the Philippines 113
    Thane, India 114
    Taipei, Taiwan 116
3. Africa 117
    Cairo, Egypt 117
    Dodoma, Tanzania 119
    Bujumbura, Burundi 120
4. Pacific 122
    Rahui-Pōkeka, New Zealand 122
5. Latin America 123
    Managua, Nicaragua 123
    Camagüey, Cuba 124

6. *Europe*   126
     Mitrovica, Kosovo   126
     Aarhus, Denmark   127

References   *131*
Index   *135*

ILLUSTRATIONS

Figures

1.1	Pitt and Napoleon Carving Up the World	5
2.1	The Tower of Babel	14
3.1	United Nations, New York	26
3.2	Palenque de San Basilio	33
4.1	Colombia merchandising	42
5.1	The Global Language System	62
5.2	Aruhuaco	63
6.1	The concentric circles of English	69
7.1	Road sign in Bosnia and Herzegovina: Oborci/ Оборци	81
7.2	Tahrir Square during the revolution/coup	83
7.3	Sarajevo library	85

Tables

5.1	Languages in the world	48
5.2	Top ten world languages	50
5.3	Top ten Power Language Index	51

ACKNOWLEDGEMENTS

I would like to express my gratitude to my friends, colleagues, students, and respondents from all over the world, who provided useful feedback and support during this project. They helped me to shape the ideas I developed in this book. Their comments, corrections, and clarifications no doubt improved my text. Responsibility for inaccuracies and mistakes remains mine, of course. I am grateful to the following people (in alphabetical order, based on their first names): Abram de Swaan, Amira Hanafi, Andrew Craddock, Ann Peckstadt, Anne Walraet, Arber Hoti, Arnel Bilibli, Arvi Ramaswami, Aura Lopez, Ayla Sileghem, Cecilie Hamnes Carlsen, Celine Haastrup, Christine Engelen, Dirk Van Overmeire, Dragana Van de moortel, Eleni Steck, Fernanda Soto, Filipa Perdigão Ribeiro, Geisa Dávila Pérez, Grégoire Verbeke, Harald E. Mabwe, Hong Ding, Jan Van Maele, Johnny Unger, Kai L. Chan, Kristof Savski, Liesse Horimbere, Louisa Semlyen, Maartje De Meulder, Mark Sebba, Michael Meeuwis, Miriam Schellen, Nazli Üstünes, Nils Van Steenkiste, Oona Van Achter, Paul Baker, Paul Kerswill, Qun Yu, Rachele Lawton, Ruth Vandewalle, Samantha Brunt, Sara Nović, Sherry Lin, Sonya Ochaney, Steven Neyrinck, Taheke Noda, Vincent D'Hondt, Zoë Teuwen. My gratitude goes as well to the Esperanto Association of Britain and *Ethnologue*, who have been willing to answer my queries. Last but not least, I would like to thank my anonymous reviewers and interviewees.

PART 1
Language is politics

1
THE LANGUAGE MYTH

> I speak Spanish to God, Italian to women, French to men, and German to my dog.
>
> (attributed to Charles V)

The invention of a myth

A couple of years ago, a Danish friend of mine asked whether I knew what the most typical Danish dish was. I wasn't quite sure what to say, but I thought *smørrebrød* was a safe bet.[1] So that's what I said. 'Wrong', she replied, 'it's *pizza*'. I was baffled, but then I realized the street where she lived was lined with pizzerias. And this was Copenhagen, not Rome. There wasn't a single place selling *smørrebrød*. Of course, this may have been due to globalization: pizza is available all over the world while *smørrebrød* is not, not even in Denmark. More importantly, the example shows that people think in clichés which may be dead but won't lie down. Language belongs to the same realm of myths. That is, not language as such, but many of the beliefs people have developed about language. For instance, the belief that one's language determines the way one thinks, that Eskimos have more than 100 words for snow, or that Danish is the ugliest language in the world (or is it Dutch?). These beliefs – or ideologies, as I will call them – don't make sense, and yet they are taken for granted.

The basic tenet of this book is that languages do not exist. Why then write a book on something that does not exist? At first sight, the whole idea appears to be absurd. My underlying assumption is that languages are in fact constructions. That is, they do not exist in the natural world, though we do speak of 'natural' languages – languages that have developed spontaneously in contrast to artificial languages or computer codes. In fact, however, a natural language is to a large extent artificial too, in that man has played a decisive role in its construction and in the way it is used. The word *man* is to be taken quite literally as most of these people were and are men indeed.

Languages are constructions in a number of ways. First of all, language can be used to construct a particular reality or *view of the world*. This is the case in, for instance, religion or politics. In his famous essay *Politics and the English Language* (1946), George Orwell focused on the way language can be used to make lies sound true.[2] For example, a government might use the term 'pacification' to justify its actions when bombarding a defenceless village. A more modern example is the term 'collateral damage', which is used in US military terminology for the killing of unintended victims during an attack. 'Collateral damage' sounds almost trivial when compared to 'killing by accident', yet the consequences are the same. Orwell's essay anticipates his development of Newspeak – a simplified language constructed to limit the range of thought – in *Nineteen Eighty-Four*.[3] Even though Orwell's belief in a dialectical relationship between language and thought might be called rather naïve, it is a compelling idea, and 'newspeak' has since become a common name for the ambiguous euphemistic language used chiefly in political propaganda.

Second, languages are used to construct *identities*, in particular the identities of nations, groups of people, and individuals. When defining their identity, people try to answer the question not only of 'Who are we?', but also of 'Who are we not?'. Thus, one's identity is dependent on the way the *other* is defined. Self- and other-identification can be observed in the names ascribed to people, their countries and their languages, and in the characteristics ascribed to them. Whereas the self is usually described in a positive way, the other is often portrayed in a negative way. For example, a people may refer to itself simply as 'the people' (e.g. *Cymry*, the Welsh word for themselves), while other people are referred to as foreigners or sometimes even as non-people. A good example is the Greek word *barbaros*, which was used to refer to all foreigners not belonging to the great Greek civilization. The word emphasizes the otherness of outsiders and their gibberish languages, which sounded like 'bar bar bar'. These origins are reflected in today's usage of the word barbarian, meaning uncivilized or primitive – the original meaning of 'foreigner' has been lost.

Last but not least, *languages are themselves constructions*. They are complex systems consisting of grammar, vocabulary, spelling, and so on. Again, these systems do not arise naturally. And languages are not only described, but also codified in books and other works of reference that prescribe their 'correct' or 'appropriate' usage. An extreme example is Orwell's Newspeak, though it is perhaps not as extreme as it seems. After all, languages are indeed manipulated to serve certain needs and ideologies. At a more fundamental level, languages are constructed to differentiate them from other languages and dialects. Language academies have been set up in various countries to regulate and control how a language is used. The role of these language regulators is highly political and driven by certain assumptions and beliefs concerning language. The *Académie française*, the French language council, is a good example of an authority that decrees what constitutes correct language, and which rules language users have to abide by. It goes without saying that the Academy's decisions are made by people (mostly elderly white men) and they do not reflect anything that could be observed in nature.

Many of the beliefs that will be discussed in this book originated in Europe, the continent which played a dominant role in the world for almost 500 years (roughly from the fifteenth to the twentieth century). European assumptions concerning race, religion, social class, gender, and so on were exported to all other continents and legitimized as universal values.[4] The Eurocentric worldview was challenged after the Second World War, when the postcolonial world took shape. Moreover, the United States had entered the international arena, shifting power from the 'old' to the 'new' world. European languages, however, continued to play a major role in the world, and one language in particular became the world's most dominant language: English.

The focus of this book is on the use of language as a constructor of identity and on the construction of languages themselves. Of course, language is not the only way to construct an identity – there are many other 'markers', such as gender, age, social class, and so on, which combine to shape the way a person speaks, dresses, and behaves. The identity of a larger entity such as a nation is constructed and visualized by means of borders and border controls, flags, uniforms, monuments, manifestations, and even the colour of street signs.[5] For instance, the colours used on the poles that support traffic lights in Flanders, the Dutch-speaking part of Belgium, were changed to mark the territorial difference between linguistic regions: the 'Belgian' colours red and white were replaced by the 'Flemish' colours black and yellow. As I will discuss later, language can play a crucial role in the construction of a nation. It is one of the most powerful means of distinguishing one nation from another, and the belief in distinct identities is ingrained through language use in

FIGURE 1.1 Pitt and Napoleon Carving Up the World (James Gillray, 1805)
Source: British Museum

state institutions, schools, churches, the mass media, and so on. This is not to say that nations are constructed out of the blue, but they are definitely less natural than is commonly assumed.

Tensions over language appear to be increasing, which may be because the belief that each nation has a single, unifying language is in decline. This belief was mainly propagated by advocates of the nation-state, a concept that is itself under pressure as it is endangered by fragmentation, a tendency which may be observed all over the world. Even in 'stable' regions such as the European Union, the nation-state is being threatened from within. In today's Spain, for instance, Catalonia is defiantly asserting its distinct culture and language as part of its long push for independence. Similar tendencies are evident in the United Kingdom, Italy, and Belgium. Language is a potent marker of identity, and one which is more tangible than race or religion. Often we cannot see where people come from or which religion they adhere to (unless they wear conspicuous signs to stress their identity, such as a headscarf or a turban), but their language (or dialect, or accent) will give them away immediately. Of course, people also switch between different languages (or accents) to highlight particular identities in particular situations.

The assumption that languages are essentially made by people ties in with the conceptualization of reality as a construction, which holds that social reality does not exist as such – it only exists in our interpretation and representation of it. The title of this chapter describes language as a myth, a widely held but false belief. The myth is created to serve a particular purpose, namely the construction of an identity. Several of the ideas in this book are inspired by Benedict Anderson, the title of whose seminal book *Imagined Communities* I have used as the title of my third chapter.[6] Anderson is not the only scholar to have established a link between language and imagined communities. Alastair Pennycook went a step further when he referred to 'the pernicious myth that language exists'.[7] Stephen May has claimed that languages are created out of the politics of state-making.[8] Thus, languages are *made* different from other languages for political purposes. Linguistic 'borders' and other identity markers are set up by means of the *politics* of vocabulary, grammar, spelling, and especially pronunciation.

The quotation given at the beginning of this chapter may also belong to the realm of myth. It has been attributed to Charles V (1500–1558), emperor of the Holy Roman Empire, a vast and multilingual empire with territories in Europe as well as in Latin America. Interestingly, the quotation exists in different versions, with different roles assigned to the languages. In other versions, the emperor speaks Italian to kings, French to women, and German or Dutch to his horse (or soldiers). In the sixteenth century, however, the divisions between languages were not as clear-cut as they are today, and it may have been difficult to tell Spanish from Portuguese, French from Italian, or German from Dutch.[9] These distinctions are more recent, as I will discuss in Chapter 3. The quotation probably dates from the seventeenth century, long after the death of the emperor. It reflects the view of Romance languages (which all derive from Latin) as the languages of high culture or nobility and Germanic languages as the languages of low culture or the common people. Another quotation often attributed to Charles V (or Carlos I, as he is known in Spanish) is 'One is worth as many people as the languages one knows'.[10] Again, it is highly questionable whether the emperor ever actually uttered these words, but the sentiment reminds us of the distinct identities afforded to individual languages.

Throughout history, writers, philosophers, and others have pondered the nature of language and attributed different characteristics to it. In her novel *Jacob's Room* (1922), Virginia Woolf describes language as 'wine upon the lips'.[11] One of the protagonists, a university lecturer, intones Latin phrases as though his words were wine (while sipping port). Samuel Johnson, the eighteenth-century English lexicographer, takes a slightly less sensual approach, describing language as 'the dress of thought', an idea which was also expressed by the Austrian-British philosopher Ludwig Wittgenstein. Many writers regard their language as the virtual home or country in which they live. Think, for instance, of French writer Albert Camus and his Portuguese counterpart Fernando Pessoa. In popular culture, too, language is often seen as the home or soul of a nation. These strong metaphors testify to the emotional content of language, as will be discussed later.

According to the French sociologist Pierre Bourdieu, language should be viewed not only as a means of communication, but also as a mechanism of power.[12] A language may be perceived as a threat to another language, which may in turn be perceived to need some kind of protection. As a result, metaphors of war are prevalent when it comes to language (for instance, the very concept of *language war*). In a global context, English is often considered a threat to other languages (hence the 'tsunami of English' metaphor), although it is sometimes seen as a solution to long-lasting language conflicts as well (e.g. in multilingual countries such as Belgium or Switzerland). In international, national, and subnational contexts, languages may vie for power, prestige, or dominance in a particular area, such as education. The terms language war, struggle or strife are mainly used in relation to conflicts in which a minority group and its language is dominated by the majority group and language. This can be observed in multilingual empires all over the world, for instance Russia or China. Yet a minority language can also be dominant if its language has more prestige or power (political, economic, cultural) than the majority language. This was the case in Finland, for example, before its independence (1917), when the power was in the hands of its Swedish-speaking minority. Another example is nineteenth-century Belgium, where the Flemish majority was dominated by the minority French-speaking elite. Dominant minorities on other continents include the Afrikaners in South Africa during the apartheid regime, the Tutsi in Rwanda, and ethnic Chinese in several countries in South East Asia.

The politics of language

This book deals with the politics of language. By politics, I do not just mean the activities of politicians and other policymakers, but also the everyday power struggles we all get involved in as members of our *polis* – by which I mean society at large rather than the original meaning of 'city' or 'city-state'. Apart from discussing language as a construction, the book addresses power relations between languages and the use of languages in particular contexts. Other important aspects of language, such as its use as a tool to manipulate people, are beyond the scope of this book. The book is written for anyone who has an interest in language, which should include most people, as almost everyone uses language. Yet not everyone is a language specialist, and many clichés about language are widely taken for granted. The book tries to debunk some of the myths about language and to put things in their proper perspective. I approach the topic not only as a linguist, but also as a language user, drawing on both my expertise and my experience with language. The approach is anecdotal in that my examples are based on the languages and language areas I am most familiar with. There may be some bias in this approach, as I am most familiar with the European context and with Germanic languages in particular. The personal language histories in this book are meant to counterbalance my somewhat Eurocentric approach, but their primary aim is to illustrate the complexities discussed above. Readers are welcome to submit their own language histories, which I plan to collect on a specially designed website.

My own language history can be summarized as follows. I grew up in Belgium, a linguistically sensitive country with a Dutch-speaking north (Flanders) and a French-speaking south (Wallonia). Both of my parents were speakers of Dutch, but my mother was from Flanders whereas my father was from the Netherlands (the differences between these two varieties of Dutch are similar to the differences between British and American English). From a very early age, I was aware of tiny linguistic and cultural differences between the two varieties, and of the fact that many people spoke other languages (most notably French). This personal language history probably stimulated my interest in languages. I majored in English and German, and then became a language teacher and researcher with a special interest in the use of English as an international language. Later, I obtained a PhD in Linguistics in the United Kingdom, combining my interest in languages and politics. I regard English as my adopted language, one which I use for personal as well as academic purposes. Apart from Dutch and English, my linguistic repertoire includes German, French, and some Spanish. These languages help me to 'understand' related languages, but I also have a keen interest in other, non-Western languages. In 1989, I lived in China for almost a year, where I picked up some Chinese, but I never managed to speak it fluently. I find it hard to be in an environment where I cannot talk to people or read anything. I think I am a reading addict as I read everything I see, including nutrition and other labels (I try to read all languages) or subtitles on television (even when I understand the language).

Every single person can be regarded as a *language manager*[13] in that she or he makes choices, either consciously or unconsciously, about how to use language. For instance, in the previous sentence I deliberately used the word order 'she or he' rather than 'he or she' to disrupt the norm and thus make a statement about gender. Many of these decisions relate to choices that are less obvious, and to our fundamental beliefs concerning language, which may not be conscious at all. For instance, if one believes that a particular language is difficult to learn, or ugly, or that it is not in fact a language in its own right, but rather a dialect of another language, these beliefs are reflected in one's approach to that particular language. Language management occurs at all levels of society, not just at the individual level. That is, institutions as diverse as governments and universities develop their own language policies based on underlying beliefs about language. These beliefs may be explicit (e.g. the decision to use English as an official language, reflecting the belief that English provides access to power or knowledge) or implicit (e.g. the belief that a certain accent is better than another, as a result of which some people may be preferred over others when applying for a job).

This type of language management plays a crucial role in narratives – in the *stories* we construct to make sense of our worlds. Often these stories are like bad movies, in which 'we' (or the ones we identify with) are the good guys and 'they' (the others) are the bad guys. These stereotypes are used to interpret the world, and to justify certain actions, including wars. In most *grand narratives* (stories that provide a comprehensive view of the world), the present is seen as a moment between the glorious past (some kind of paradise) and the future (another type of heaven), in which the glorious past will be re-established. In order to convey all this, strong imagery is used to paint pictures in our minds or create a certain atmosphere (e.g. in fairy tales, prayers, and political speeches). Language is the magic that conjures up the imagery and the cement which binds the narratives together. Without it, they would simply fall apart.

As we have seen, power relations between people are expressed through and reflected in language. Therefore, *language is politics*. This book deals with the politics of language, and it is organized as a journey through space and time. While it doesn't purport to be complete, it does aim to present a fair picture of a variety of linguistic landscapes from both the past and the present, and to describe some possible future trends. The book consists of two separate parts. The first part has nine chapters organized as follows: Chapters 1 and 2 deal with the mythification of language and its origin; Chapters 3 and 4 discuss how people imagine themselves through language and how they construct language; Chapters 5 and 6 focus on world languages, with English as the ultimate world language; and Chapters 7 and 8 cover languages and war, as well as their life and death. Chapter 9 draws all of these ideas together, and argues in favour of a balanced or ecological attitude towards language. The second, shorter part of the book presents 11 language histories in which individual contributors from all over the world reflect on their personal language practices. While these personal language practices illustrate some of the concepts discussed in the first part, they should primarily be understood as individual narratives.

As the purpose of this book is to debunk some of the most common myths regarding language, I'd like to take the opportunity to introduce some of these myths briefly here:

1. *Language A is more beautiful than language B*. 'Beautiful' can be replaced by any other adjective you can think of: complex, difficult, expressive, poetic, rational,

refined, romantic, sensual, and so on. One could also say that language A is better suited to education, to making love (or war), to singing, or to whatever other purpose. The bottom line is that these clichés tend to reflect someone's perceptions or aspirations rather than reality. A good example is the irrationality with which Antoine de Rivarol, an eighteenth-century French writer, claimed that French was the most rational language in the world.

2. *A language is superior to a dialect.* This is a tricky one, as a language (especially a 'standard' language) is often far more powerful than a dialect: it is propagated by the authorities (states, schools, the media) and thus granted a superior status, while a dialect is commonly regarded as inferior. We should realize, however, that a language is nothing more than a dialect which has achieved a special status. Thus, a language has the power a dialect lacks. To put it another way, 'a language is a dialect with an army and a fleet', as will be discussed in Chapter 4.

3. *Language is typical of humans, not animals.* It all depends on how we define language, but it should be pointed out that language ability is not peculiar to humans and that it can be observed in other species as well. Song-learning birds may be a particularly good example. On the other hand, humans use language in a more abstract way than animals. Think, in particular, of our ability to tell stories, which may range from lullabies to philosophical treatises.

4. *Language determines thought.* This is a commonly held belief, yet it is absurd, as there is no scientific evidence that the language you speak determines what you think. There is no proof that a French mind thinks any differently from a German mind, even though this is what many people actually believe. It may be more appropriate to argue that people do not think in their native languages at all, but in a more abstract way, as argued by the cognitive psychologist Steven Pinker.[14]

5. *One's language determines one's identity.* This is an argument often heard in nationalist discourses, which typically establish close links between a particular language and an identity, especially a national identity. While language may indeed be a marker of one's identity (though not necessarily of a national identity), it certainly isn't the only marker. Race, religion, and social class (to name just a few) may also create a sense of belonging or even serve as the foundation of one's identity.

6. *English is a threat to other languages.* This may indeed be true, but it could be true of any language. It all depends on who has the power and who does not. In today's world, English is the most widely spoken language, and those who have access to English have access to power in the world, whether political, economic, or cultural. While this dominance may be detrimental to other languages, it may also create opportunities for better communication and even access to other languages and cultures. Last but not least, it should be noted that there are many places in the world where English is not spoken at all.

7. *Chinese is the language of the future.* Or: we should all start learning Chinese instead of English, as China is about to become the most powerful nation in

the world. China's economic power may be undeniable, but it seems unlikely that Chinese will take over the role of English in the world. Apart from the complexity of the language, there are also pragmatic reasons for adopting English rather than Chinese as the world's lingua franca: at present, there are far more Chinese people who speak English than there are speakers of other languages who speak Chinese. Very few speakers of English speak Chinese.

8. *When a language dies, a culture dies.* Though this is what many people believe, it is not necessarily true: even when a language dies, a culture can stay alive. In fact, this has happened many times throughout the ages. In many parts of the world, people do not speak their 'original' languages anymore, but their culture is alive and kicking. A good example may be black culture in the United States, which uses English as its mode of expression. Culture can live on in other elements, such as food, dance, and so on, since language is just one aspect of culture.

9. *We should pay more attention to speaking and writing in a correct way.* Or: we can no longer write or speak 'proper' English (or French, or German, or whatever language). This is a common complaint. The question, however, is: What is correct language? Who makes the rules? The obsession with 'correct' language assumes the existence of some kind of divine rules, which hold true once and for all. But this view does not take into account the fact that language changes, and so do its rules. What was considered correct in the past may not be correct today, and today's rules may not be tomorrow's rules.

10. *The more languages you speak, the more human you are.* I wish it were true. While speaking several languages can help you to understand more people, both literally and figuratively, it is highly questionable whether it actually makes you more 'human'. A polyglot may be a mass murderer, after all.

While there may be some truth in each of these clichés, none of them really bears up to scrutiny, despite being repeated time and again. I will discuss some of them in more detail in the chapters that follow.

Notes

1 *Smørrebrød* is an open sandwich, usually consisting of a piece of buttered rye bread and a topping of fish or meat, cheese or spreads.
2 Orwell (1946).
3 Orwell (1949).
4 Bauman and Briggs (2003: 67–68).
5 Billig (1995) referred to these everyday representations of the nation as 'banal nationalism'.
6 Anderson (1983).
7 Pennycook (2006: 67).
8 May (2006: 260).
9 De Grauwe (1999). See: http://hdl.handle.net/1854/LU-110387 (in Dutch). One of the few texts in English on this topic is an older article by C.A.J. Armstrong (1965, 1983: 386–409).

10 In Latin, the language of high culture at that time, the quotation reads: '*Tot linguas calles tot homines vales*'.
11 Woolf (1922: 34).
12 Bourdieu (1991).
13 Spolsky (2004: 8) uses the term *language management* to refer to interventions by a *language manager* (e.g. a legislative assembly) in a particular language situation.
14 Pinker (1994: 44).

2
THE ORIGIN OF LANGUAGE

Colourless green ideas

While I am writing these sentences, it is still dark outside and the birds in my garden are singing their early morning songs. What are they singing? Are they *saying* anything? Can only humans speak? What is the origin and nature of language? These and other questions are the focus of this chapter.

The origin of language and the question of why people speak different languages has been the topic of scholarly discussions for many centuries. However, achieving consensus has proven impossible, mainly because of the lack of direct evidence. This may explain why so many myths and other stories have grown up around the topic. One of the earliest attempts to explain why people speak different languages is the Tower of Babel, a biblical story from the Book of Genesis. The story goes that people all used to speak the same language, until one day they agreed to build a tower that would be tall enough to reach heaven. To thwart their plans, God then gave them different languages to make sure they could no longer understand each other, and scattered them around the world. The word babel from the story's title derives from the Hebrew *balal*, which means 'to jumble' or 'to confuse'. In English, the word survives in *babble* (i.e. talk rapidly, often in an incomprehensible way). In Dutch, a language closely related to English, the verb *babbelen* means 'to chat'.

Similar accounts of the origin of language can be found in mythologies all over the world. Many of these myths refer to floods and catastrophes which caused populations to become scattered all over the world. One such account is an Aztec story which exists in different versions but whose essence remains the same in all of them. In the story, only one man, Coxcox, and one woman, Xochiquetzal, survive a global flood. They have many children, but none of them are able to speak. They are endowed with language when a dove arrives, sent by the great spirit. Unfortunately,

14 Language is politics

FIGURE 2.1 The Tower of Babel (Pieter Bruegel the Elder, 1563)

they cannot understand one another as they are given different languages. These languages represent all the different languages spoken throughout the world.

It should be pointed out that assumptions and theories concerning language inevitably reflect the *politics around language* – that is, all ideas are rooted in a particular historical, cultural, social, and political context. While complex linguistic theories and the diversity of thought they reflect cannot be dealt with in detail here, I will focus on two groundbreaking theories and the controversies they created: the idea of a universal grammar and the idea that language determines thought.

In Darwinian terms, language may be understood as an evolutionary adaptation and as the product of a carefully engineered biological instinct. According to Noam Chomsky,[1] one of the founders of modern linguistics and a well-known political activist, language is an evolutionary development unique to the human species. Chomsky rejects earlier behaviourist views which regard the mind as a blank slate, arguing instead that all humans share an underlying linguistic structure, which is biologically determined and genetically transmitted. The sentence 'Colourless green ideas sleep furiously', which Chomsky used in his 1957 book *Syntactic Structures*, demonstrates the distinction between syntax and semantics. While the sentence is nonsensical from a semantic point of view, it is grammatically correct. According to Chomsky, humans are born with an innate 'universal grammar', as a result of which they can acquire the ability to understand and produce language. A human child learns to understand and produce an infinite number of entirely new sentences, but a kitten will never acquire this ability. Steven Pinker,[2] the author of *The Language Instinct*, agrees with the Chomskyan idea of a universal grammar, but not with the notion that evolutionary theory can explain the human language instinct. In calling language an instinct, Pinker makes the point that language is not a human invention like metalworking or even writing, but rather an innate human ability comparable to the instinct of a spider weaving webs.

The ideas developed by Chomsky and Pinker are not undisputed, and they too may belong to the realm of myths. According to the British linguist Vyvyan Evans,[3] language does *not* arise from a so-called universal grammar. This is what he calls 'the old view', a view which is still alive and kicking despite being wrong. Chomsky's views on language are taught at universities worldwide and widely sanctioned by textbooks which are compulsory reading for today's students. Evans adds that he was also trained using these textbooks, and the same holds for me. He points out that the language-as-instinct thesis is a language myth which reflects the zeitgeist of the second half of the twentieth century, an extreme form of rationalism. I agree with Evans that the thesis is merely speculative linguistics, not based on actual findings. The view that language is innate and that there is some kind of universal grammar may be attractive, but it is also far-fetched. Since Chomsky's and Pinker's books appeared, science has moved on, and their speculative view has been largely disproved: there is no universal grammar, and language is not innate. While it cannot be disputed that human children are biologically prepared for language (i.e. they are neurobiologically equipped to acquire language in a way no other species is), the idea that a universal grammar is present at birth must be rejected. Instead, as Evans argues, it is our species-specific *cultural intelligence* which facilitates intersubjective communication. In other words, we learn language through painstaking practice and trial and error. This is what Evans calls the language-as-use thesis.

Because of their cultural intelligence, humans are able to conceptualize and organize the world they live in. In contrast to most other species, which have to struggle for their survival, humans (or at least some of them) can make a decent living. This luxury is thanks to the invention of farming some 10,000 years ago, as a result of which humans were freed from hunting and gathering and could organize themselves in entirely different ways. Humans invented world religions (God was created by man, not the other way round), great philosophies, and social, political, and economic systems in order to organize societies and to make sense of their own existence. Language inevitably played a crucial role in the dissemination of these ideologies: think of the invention and development of writing and, much later, the use of radio, television, and social media. Language is therefore more than a mere instinct or the reflection of an innate 'universal grammar'. While human language is the result of a long process of evolution in a Darwinian sense, it is cultural intelligence which has helped humans to shape the world as we know it today. In short, language made us human, but humans made language too.

What happens if a child is raised by animals and is eliminated from social interaction with other humans? While it is impossible to set up such an experiment for ethical reasons, so-called 'wild children' nevertheless feature prominently in our imagination. One such story is the case of Dina Sanichar, a 6-year-old boy who was raised by wolves in the Indian jungle of Uttar Pradesh in 1872. After hunters captured the boy (and killed the wolves), he was brought to a mission-run orphanage. Apparently, Dina behaved like a wolf in all respects – he despised wearing clothes, ate raw meat only, and sharpened his teeth on bones. Even more importantly, he appeared not to have any capacity for language, making animal noises instead.[4] Even though this and other similar stories can hardly be verified, they seem to confirm the thesis that language is not innate, but rather acquired by use from infancy onwards.

Another issue that has been studied widely relates to the link between language and thinking. Perhaps the most well-known theory is the Sapir–Whorf hypothesis, named after Edward Sapir, an American anthropologist and linguist, and his protégé Benjamin Lee Whorf, a chemical engineer by profession who had developed an interest in linguistics. The 'strong version' of the Sapir–Whorf hypothesis holds that language determines thought – in other words, that the way people think is determined by the categories made available by their language. This implies that people who speak different languages also think differently. Unfortunately, the hypothesis is based on limited and poorly analysed samples. Moreover, Whorf tended towards mysticism, which did not improve the quality of his analysis. In short, there is no evidence that language shapes one's way of thinking. That is, we think not in language, but in more abstract media of thought. Those who believe that the language we speak affects and reflects our view of the world often give as an example the number of words that Eskimo languages have for snow. Yet the idea that Eskimos[5] have an unusually large number of words for snow is itself a common myth. Depending on the source, the number of words may be inflated to 50 or even 100. The problem is that a lot depends on how one defines 'word' and 'word root', as many of these so-called words in fact derive from other words. This can be illustrated by an example in English: *snow* and *snowy* are separate words, but the -y in the adjective *snowy* shows that the word is derived from the word root *snow*. To sum up, language and thinking are clearly related, but the hypothesis of linguistic determinism is now generally agreed to be false.

As regards the function of language, one may argue that language developed as a system for communicating basic needs or messages (e.g. regarding food or danger). As communities grew larger and more complex, communication became more complex too. Thus, language needs reflect the complexity of a society. As societies become more complex, the ways in which people and their habitats or territories are organized need some kind of standardization (think of governmental and other institutions, the economy, military, education, and so on). Likewise, a standardized language is needed to make efficient and large-scale communication possible. In our modern world, some languages are used by very small communities, whereas others are used in several countries and even across continents. We might say that

English is the most 'successful' language as it covers almost the entire world. The next two sections discuss the differences between so-called natural and artificial languages and between human and animal languages.

Natural and artificial languages

Simply put, a natural language has developed naturally, whereas an artificial language has been devised for a particular purpose. Yet this difference between natural and artificial language is rather ... artificial. Natural languages are also artificial, to a certain extent, as languages typically go through a long process of engineering, including the introduction of all kinds of prescriptive rules concerning spelling, grammar, and vocabulary (see Chapter 4). Many of these rules can be called artificial in that they are clearly devised to serve a particular purpose (e.g. communication over a larger area), and they can hardly be called natural. On the other hand, some artificial languages – such as Esperanto – may be regarded as natural languages in that they can be learned in a natural way, for instance if children grow up speaking Esperanto as their first language. To sum up, all languages are primarily *made* by people, and they are less natural than they may appear at first sight. Moreover, as pointed out earlier, the borders between languages are artificial, and so are the borders between languages and dialects. In the following paragraphs, I discuss three languages which show that the distinction between natural and artificial languages does not hold: sign language, Esperanto, and Basic English.

Sign language

A sign language is a natural language with its own grammar and vocabulary. It is not based on speech, but instead makes use of visual and manual signs. Even though signs can reflect gestures which can be understood easily (e.g. when signing 'hello'), usually their meanings are not so obvious – which makes them very similar to words in spoken language.[6] Grammatical features such as questions, plurals, tenses, and gender can also be signed. Like in spoken language, the grammar of sign languages is governed by rules which have to be learned. Contrary to popular belief, a sign language is not more artificial than a spoken language. Until the 1960s, it was widely believed that signing was detrimental to the language acquisition of deaf children, as a result of which these children were sometimes physically punished. Moreover, sign languages were not regarded as 'real' languages, resulting in a long and bitter struggle for equal rights. From the 1970s onwards, sign language came to be more readily accepted as a means of communication. An increasing number of countries now recognize sign languages and they are also being used more widely on television, at conferences, and so on. In 2006, New Zealand was the first country to promote its sign language (New Zealand Sign Language, NZSL) as a national language, alongside English and Maori. In reality, however, English is clearly dominant, and the official recognition of NZSL and Maori is merely symbolic. That is, NZSL and Maori are used for specific events, but they do not have the same impact or 'power' as English in society at large.

Sign languages come in standard varieties and in dialects, which makes them very similar to spoken languages. Whereas many spoken languages do not respect national borders, sign languages are more or less confined to these borders. For instance, English-speaking countries such as the United States and the United Kingdom have their own sign languages (American Sign Language, ASL, and British Sign Language, BSL, respectively). The same holds for other countries which have their own sign languages, even though their spoken languages are used beyond their borders (e.g. German and French). ASL is often used in an international context, mirroring the use of spoken English as a lingua franca. Black American Sign Language (BASL), a dialect of ASL and a holdover from school segregation, is used most commonly by deaf African Americans in the United States.

Even though deafness is commonly perceived to be some kind of disability, deaf people regard it as part of their identity. Thus, deafness becomes a matter of *language difference*.[7] In other words, being deaf is like belonging to an ethnic group which has its own language, and therefore the Deaf community is best understood as a unique minority linguistic group. This is even reflected in the spelling of the word *deaf* adopted by the Deaf community: when spelt with a small letter, it refers to an audiological state, while *Deaf* (with a capital D) refers to a cultural identity.[8] Deaf people also disagree with medical professionals who regard loss of hearing as a problem which has to be fixed. According to the Deaf, nothing has to be fixed at all. This also explains the deep controversy regarding the cochlear implant, an electronic medical device that replaces the function of the damaged inner ear. While the cochlear implant is often described as a miracle device that will eliminate deafness, the Deaf tend to see it as a technological artefact that threatens their Deaf culture and identity.[9] These two ideological positions are almost incompatible. According to Deaf activists, the cochlear implant reflects society's intolerance of difference and its tendency towards medicalization. This is a view they share with other minority groups, such as civil rights, LGBT, and feminist movements, who champion similar ways of thinking about differences.

According to Sara Nović, an American writer and Deaf activist, her deafness offers her a unique perspective on the world, which explains why she does not want a cochlear implant.[10] Instead, she uses a combination of ASL, her own voice, and lip-reading. She summarizes her position succinctly as follows: 'I like being Deaf'.[11] As a Deaf person, she says she pays more attention to the visual components of the world and is less distracted than the average hearing person. Or, in her own words, she's not constantly shoving headphones over her ears to cut herself off from her fellow humans. As she perceives it, she can enjoy a 'protective bubble of silence' while at the same time being fully engaged with the world around her. She describes the Deaf community as a supportive community which is generally less discriminatory – perhaps because they know what it is like to be discriminated against.

Even though deaf people cannot listen to music, they can enjoy it as they can feel the vibrations of the music being played. This also explains why there are deaf composers, a good contemporary example being the Scottish virtuoso percussionist Evelyn Glennie, who was initially rejected entrance to the Royal Academy of Music because of her deafness. She demonstrates that listening to music involves more than sound waves hitting one's eardrums, and that deaf people can be excellent musicians indeed.[12] What this tells us is that sign language is a living language which can be used for all purposes other languages can be used for, including performing poetry and making music.

Esperanto

Esperanto (literally 'one who hopes') is the most widely spoken artificial language in the world. According to *Ethnologue*, the catalogue of world languages, Esperanto is spoken by some 2 million speakers. Even though Esperanto was conceived as an apolitical language, its underlying commitment can be called highly political. The language was constructed in 1887 by L.L. Zamenhoff, a Polish-Jewish ophthalmologist who spoke several languages. Zamenhoff had grown up in a multilingual environment and realized there was a lot of tension between speakers of different languages. As Zamenhoff saw it, the tensions were due to the fact that these speakers lacked a common language. He therefore created Esperanto, with the aim of smoothing over the uneasy coexistence of different languages and cultures. Zamenhoff wanted to make a language which would be easy to learn, politically neutral, and truly international. From a contemporary perspective, however, Esperanto can hardly be called international, as it is mainly based on the European languages Zamenhoff was familiar with. While its vocabulary derives from Romance and Germanic languages, its grammar is based on Slavic languages. As a result, learning Esperanto is not so easy for speakers of non-European languages, and as a European language it is definitely not politically neutral. This means the claim that Esperanto could be an alternative to the growing use of English throughout the world may not be valid. It is not entirely clear why Esperanto has never really taken off as a world language, but it has been argued that the fact that Esperanto is not culturally embedded may have something to do with it. After all, Esperanto lacks the grand narratives (myths, great literature) which may make it less attractive to language learners who want more than a purely 'functional' language. In any case, it clearly doesn't have the same level of appeal as English, a language whose presence is conspicuous all over the world.

What makes Esperanto really unique in comparison to other languages is the way it has been promoted as a tool for creating a better society, as laid out in the 1996 *Prague Manifesto*.[13] The manifesto embraces democratic communication, global education, effective language learning, multilingualism, language rights, language diversity, and human emancipation as its founding principles. As Esperanto stresses equality among languages, it is not intended to replace anyone's native language. Indeed, the Esperanto website provides information in 66 languages, including some minority languages such as Occitan.[14] There is a vibrant community of Esperanto speakers across the globe, and hundreds of Esperanto organizations. One of these organizations is the Esperanto Association of Britain (*Asocio de Britio* in Esperanto).[15] One of the members of the association, a native speaker of English who also speaks French and Italian and a smattering of some other languages, told me he uses Esperanto every day. He learned Esperanto out of curiosity more than 15 years ago, but does not consider it part of his identity. His attitude could be called rather pragmatic. While he does not dispute that English comes closest to claiming the title of *the* international language, he points out that there are many places in the world where English is of no use whatsoever. What he finds unique about Esperanto is the fact that it was planned, and also that it has seen such a spectacular growth in its speaker base since 1887. Half-jokingly, he adds that he and his partner sometimes use Esperanto as a secret language if they want to talk privately in public.[16] Another member, who started learning Esperanto at the age of 15, largely takes the same pragmatic attitude. The main reason why he learned Esperanto was that he was interested in the idea of a constructed language. As Esperanto does not have complex rules, he feels more confident in it than in German or French. He also likes Esperanto music, of which he has a good collection. Esperanto is his 'niche hobby', but is not part of his identity either. Or, in his own words, Esperanto is 'something I do, not something I am'.[17] This attitude is very different from the Deaf community's, in which sign language is an essential part of their identity.

For speakers of Esperanto, Esperanto *can* be part of their identity, and some of them see it as an important part indeed. As one of them replied, '*esperanto ja estas parto de mia identeco*' ('Esperanto is part of my identity') – to which the speaker added that he considers everything about himself to be part of his identity, including the colour of his hair and skin, the languages he speaks, and the books he has read. This view of identity is what he calls '*kompleta priskribo*' (a 'complete description'). As a consequence, Esperanto is *not* just something he does, but which has opened his mind to many things, not just the language itself. In his view, the original aim of Esperanto – to allow people of different cultures to communicate in a neutral language while preserving the distinct cultures and languages of the world – is something we still sorely need.[18] Other speakers of Esperanto take an activist attitude, which may remind one of the Deaf community: 'Esperanto is not a hobby for me – it's a specific, clear program for action'. The latter speaker sees Esperanto as a solution for the problems faced by people who live in a monocultural and monolingual world.[19]

Basic English

Unlike Esperanto, Basic English has its roots in a single language and serves only a limited number of domains. Hence the name Basic, which stands for British, American, Scientific, International, and Commercial. Basic English was created in 1930 by the linguist and philosopher Charles Kay Ogden as an international auxiliary language as well as an aid for teaching English as a second language. The purposes underlying Basic English and Esperanto are quite similar, as both were intended to promote peace, though both failed to live up to this purpose. It was the Allied victory in the Second World War that triggered the interest in a simplified form of English as a means of world peace. Today, Basic English survives mainly as the 850-word list which is used as a beginner's vocabulary of English taught worldwide. According to readability expert Rudolf Flesch,[20] however, Basic English is not basic, and neither is it English. As the vocabulary is too restricted, texts look awkward and are more difficult to read than necessary. Flesch points out that the elimination of words and the simplification of grammar produce a maze of bizarre circumlocutions. For instance, a simple sentence such as 'Meet my cousin Mary' would become 'Come across my father's sister's daughter' in Basic English.[21]

George Orwell was initially a proponent of Basic English, but later became critical of it. In fact, Basic English inspired his introduction of Newspeak in the dystopian novel *Nineteen Eighty-Four*. Orwell's Newspeak is a controlled language with a limited vocabulary and restricted grammar, designed to limit freedom of thought. In Newspeak, the very word 'free' can only be used in sentences such as 'This dog is free from lice', and not in the sense of 'politically free', since the concept of freedom no longer exists. Euphemisms are widely used, for instance *goodthink* (to think in an orthodox manner) and *Minipax* (an abbreviation for the Ministry of Peace, which is actually the ministry responsible for *war*). The latter examples are reminiscent of real-life words such as Nazi (national socialism) or Comintern (communist international). In Orwell's dystopia, language and thought are tightly controlled by Big Brother, the figurehead of the totalitarian state in which every citizen is under constant surveillance. Newspeak makes unorthodox thinking simply impossible.[22] As observed earlier, Orwell's deterministic link between language and thought may be rather naïve, yet his hauntingly dystopian nightmare convincingly shows that language can be a powerful tool for manipulating people.

Animal talk

Humans do not generally understand the noises that dogs or other animals make, except for a number of common signals such as 'take me for a walk'. We can understand the sadness, happiness, and other emotions expressed by our beloved pet, but we may not interpret this form of communication as language. But maybe our dog is thinking the same about us: some of our signals make sense (e.g. sit!), but the rest of our noises may just be barking. The problem is that we cannot translate between dog and human. This is what David Bellos,[23] a British translator, refers to as 'the unbridgeable gulf between our species and others'. We could only know for sure whether animals use languages or not if we were able to solve this problem of translatability between species.

What we commonly refer to as language is the form of communication that can be spoken (voiced) and heard. The actual sound of spoken language is referred to as *speech*. This characterisation may apply to some types of animal communication as well, even though the words 'speech' and 'spoken' are usually used only in relation to human language. In biological terms, the vocal folds (commonly known as vocal cords) are responsible for phonation (i.e. the process of producing the voice). The vocal folds are housed in the larynx (or 'voice box'), an organ situated in the neck. In adult humans, the larynx is descended in the neck, a position that allows us to produce sounds. The human species is not unique in this respect, as dogs, goats, and pigs also lower their larynxes to emit calls. Apart from speech, language can also be written and read, or signed of course. While this is the case with human language, it does not hold for animal language, unless one takes into account other types of reading, such as the 'reading' of footprints. However, footprints can hardly said to be 'written', as writing involves some kind of conscious act.

Most people inevitably think of language as *human* language (i.e. a system of communication used by human beings). This view ties in with Noam Chomsky's thesis that only humans have language. Yet it is a thesis that has not gone unchallenged, and various attempts have been made to demonstrate that animals have language too. Of course, this also depends on how language is defined, but let us assume that language is the ability to convey meaning by means of vocalizations (words and sounds), signs, or gestures. Many animals communicate in different ways (e.g. through scent and smell), but the mode of communication which comes closest to human speech is auditory communication. Many animals communicate through vocalization, which applies to birds as well as mammals. Whales, the largest mammals on Earth, use so-called whale songs to communicate. The songs come in different dialects, depending on the region the whales live in.[24] The best-known form of visual communication used by animals involves gestures. Some apes have been taught to use sign language to communicate with humans.

Nim Chimpsky (an obvious pun on Noam Chomsky) was the chimpanzee subject of a study on animal language acquisition. The study was conceived in the 1970s as a challenge to Chomsky's thesis that only humans have language. Even though Nim managed to learn some American Sign Language, the data did not prove that the chimp understood language in the Chomskyan sense (i.e. as the ability to apply innate grammatical rules). The question of whether chimpanzees can understand and learn sign language remains controversial. It is difficult to prove whether apes acquire and develop language skills through natural social interactions or whether their use of language results from behavioural conditioning, in which case they use language primarily as a means of obtaining rewards.[25]

Orangutans can learn sign language too. Chantek, one of the first apes to learn sign language, died in 2017. He also learned to clean his room, to make and use tools, and to memorise the route to a fast-food restaurant.[26] However, this may be considered rather 'unnatural' behaviour for an ape. Orangutans living in the wild communicate in a different way, in that they use kiss-like sounds to convey messages. These so-called 'kiss squeaks' are produced by the action of the lips, tongue, and jaw rather than the voice, and may be compared to consonants in human speech. In recent research, more than 4,000 kiss squeaks from 48 orangutans in four wild populations were recorded and analysed. For humans, these sounds are difficult to understand, as we combine consonants and vowels to produce speech. Yet it has been argued that the study of the apes' consonant-like calls may reveal a crucial building block in the evolution of language.[27]

It goes without saying that animals use complex means of communication, and there may be some good arguments to call this language. Animals can speak, and not only in fairy tales. They have their own languages and dialects: wolves from different regions howl in different fashions, for instance. The howls of European wolves are more protracted and melodious than those of North American wolves, whose howls are louder and have a stronger emphasis on the first syllable. Yet the two are mutually intelligible, and wolves from one region can communicate with wolves from the other region. In more human terms, one could say that they speak different varieties of the same language, like British and American English. Of course, this is still a far cry from the language the wolf speaks to Little Red Riding Hood and in other fairy tales. In these stories, the wolf speaks and behaves like a human being.

The songs of birds may be closer to human language than the vocalizations of wolves and other mammals. It is well known that birds learn calls and that there are many dialects in birds' languages. Irene Pepperberg,[28] an American scientist noted for her studies of animal cognition, attempted to demonstrate that the vocal behaviour of parrots has the same characteristics as human language, and that it is more than just vocal mimicry. According to Pepperberg, the parrot she worked with, Alex, could differentiate meaning from syntax, the underlying tenet being that humans do not hold the monopoly on complex or abstract communication. Of course, her results remain controversial, and critics have claimed that Alex had merely been taught a script. It is also worth bearing in mind that not all parrots may be as clever as Alex.

Other animals, such as bees, do not use vocalizations at all, yet their ways of communicating are equally complex. For instance, western honey bees perform a dance on their return to the hive. One form of this dance, which is known as the waggle dance, indicates that food is farther away, while another, shorter dance, known as the round dance, indicates that food is nearby. The question remains, however, whether these forms of communication among apes, wolves, whales, parrots, and bees can be called languages. As humans, we cannot help but think of language as a highly complex system used by our own species, the origins of which we do not completely understand (and which, as we have seen, might be based on some kind of innate grammar). We use language to express ourselves and to communicate with other people. We use and shape languages to organize large communities, and we learn the languages of other communities. We make use of language to create art and to pursue our dreams. From this perspective, the communication systems used by non-humans appear to be merely instinctual. Indeed, not a single animal has produced a Shakespeare or Goethe – that we know of, of course. We do not yet understand the full complexity of communication among animals. It remains an open question whether human language is really unique, as Chomsky claims, or whether we should be more modest in our assumptions about the linguistic uniqueness of our own species.

Notes

1. Chomsky (1957).
2. Pinker (1994).
3. Evans (2016).
4. See: https://timeline.com/dina-sanichar-feral-children-ea9f5f3a80b2 (accessed 29 June 2019).
5. The word Eskimo is often perceived as pejorative (especially in Canada and Greenland), and has therefore been replaced by the term Inuit.
6. Signing 'hello' in American Sign Language (ASL) and other examples can be watched at: www.youtube.com/watch?v=Raa0vBXA8OQ (accessed 1 July 2019).
7. Mauldin (2016: 52).
8. Mauldin (2016: 179, note 2).
9. Mauldin (2016: 157).
10. Nović (2018a) See: www.nytimes.com/2018/11/21/opinion/deaf-cochlear-implants-sign-language.html (accessed 4 January 2019).
11. Sara Nović, personal communication, 13 January 2019. As an American with roots in Croatia, she considers this legacy part of her identity too. For a discussion of these different identities, see: http://lithub.com/writing-your-way-back-home/ (accessed 4 January 2019). In her startling novel *Girl at War*, Nović describes the impact of the war in Croatia on a young girl's coming of age.
12. Evelyn Glennie demonstrating her virtuosity: www.ted.com/talks/evelyn_glennie_shows_how_to_listen?language=en. (accessed 20 January 2019).
13. See: http://uea.org/teko/praga_manifesto_angla (accessed 18 February 2019).
14. See: http://esperanto.net/en/ (accessed 18 February 2019).
15. See: http://esperanto.org.uk and http://esperanto.org.uk/forums/ (accessed 18 February 2019).
16. Personal communication, 13 February 2019.
17. Personal communication, 16 February 2019.
18. Personal communication, 24 May 2019.
19. See discussion on Lernu: http://lernu.net/en/forumo/temo/18713 (accessed 8 March 2019).
20. Flesch (1944: 339–343).
21. Flesch (1944: 342).
22. Orwell (1949). See 'Appendix: The Principles of Newspeak'.
23. See: http://bigthink.com/videos/do-dogs-speak-human-2 (accessed 12 October 2018).
24. Whitehead and Rendall (2015).
25. Linden (1987).
26. See: www.bbc.com/news/world-us-canada-40858040 (accessed 20 February 2019).
27. Knight (2015). See: http://jeb.biologists.org/content/218/6/813.1.full (accessed 9 February 2017). See also: www.bbc.com/news/science-environment-38907681 (accessed 20 February 2019).
28. Pepperberg (2002).

3
IMAGINED COMMUNITIES

Language and identity

Identity has become a central concept in the social sciences and humanities. There are many markers of identity, such as gender, religion, social class, and so on, but the focus of this book is on how language functions as a marker of identity. This chapter discusses how people identify with particular languages and how they are used to cement communities. The link between language and national identity is relatively recent, and can be traced back to nineteenth-century Europe, where emerging modern states were trying to establish new identities. Language played a crucial role in this process. European nations, which regarded themselves as the centre of the world, even managed to establish their identities beyond the borders of their own continent. In their scramble for colonies, European powers drew imaginary lines to demarcate zones which they claimed belonged to them, and where European languages were then imposed. These borders reflected the needs (and greed) of European powers, not those of local nations. These days, linguistic and cultural identities are debated widely, mainly in the context of globalization and the emergence of multicultural societies, and in response to the perceived need to protect a 'native' identity.

The linkage between language and identity can be understood in the wider context of nationalism and the construction of nations or, as the political scientist and historian Benedict Anderson calls them, 'imagined political communities'.[1] According to Anderson, a nation is *imagined* since members of such a sizeable community will never know most of their fellow members because of the sheer size of the community, yet the image of their communion lives in the mind of each (for instance, because they share the same stories about their history). In his seminal work *Imagined Communities*, Anderson points out the importance of print capitalism (the convergence of capitalism and print technology) which made it possible for people to think about themselves in profoundly new ways – that is, in terms of imagined communities. Language has a particular capacity for generating imagined communities and hence nation-building. For instance, when young conscripts joined the army in early nineteenth-century Europe, it would have been the first time that many of them left their villages and heard languages other than their local dialects. As Anderson argues, the use of a standard language in the educational system and in the media has a similar effect of generating an imagined community.

A nation is not to be confused with a nation-state, which is a fundamental unit of world political organization. In more concrete terms, a nation-state is a sovereign state with a seat in the United Nations. A nation, on the other hand, is not a sovereign state, but its people share a heritage, including myths and memories, and a territory – which may be a historical territory, if the people are now dispersed across different states. The Kurds, for example, are the largest stateless nation in the world, with a population scattered over several countries, including Turkey, Iran, Iraq, and Syria.[2] Nations may also develop into nation-states, a process we are now observing in Scotland, Catalonia, and Flanders, to mention just a few examples in Europe. In all three cases, language plays an important role in the process of state-building.[3]

FIGURE 3.1 United Nations, New York
Source: Rachele Lawton

Contrary to popular belief, neither nations nor languages are 'natural' phenomena. Benedict Anderson has often been credited with debunking this myth, but many other writers have expressed similar views. The philosopher and social anthropologist Ernest Gellner,[4] for instance, stressed the impact of industrialization on the rise of nationalism: it was in the transition from traditional agrarian societies to modern industrial societies that nationalism developed. Whereas in the former a wide variety of languages and dialects were spoken and literacy was limited to a small elite, the latter required cultural and linguistic homogeneity. Therefore, the use of a standardized, dominant language was imposed to run society efficiently.

The views expressed by Anderson and others met with considerable resistance. Israeli professor Azar Gat[5] argues that this 'modernist' interpretation is too simplistic and too Eurocentric. According to Gat, nations and nationalism did not originate in Europe and are also much older than the nineteenth century. Moreover, he believes that Anderson's focus on European book printing as the driving force behind nation-building is misleading, as the relation between written and spoken language is far more complex than assumed by Anderson. As Gat sees it, the link between language and community dates back thousands of years and was very much part of oral traditions in many parts of the world. Consequently, what happened in Europe in the nineteenth and twentieth centuries was just the tip of the iceberg. The fact does remain, however, that language can be a crucial factor in the construction of identities (both individual and collective) and that language and nationalism are often closely linked, especially in today's world.

Language ideologies

Language and literature have the power to shape and reshape realities. Myths, which typically belong to the realm of oral literature, help us to imagine our communities. In ancient Egypt, for instance, the pharaoh was considered to be a god. However, the imagined godlike ruler did also exist tangibly in the world and reigned supreme by virtue of the stories that were told and retold by millions of people in the Nile Valley. Much of the written literature produced in later centuries served a similar purpose: countless tales recount the heroic deeds of chiefs and kings and the births of their nations. Many of these stories have entered both the individual and collective psyches, and they have found their way into poems and other literary accounts, many of which have become classics. Unfortunately, these stories can also be detrimental, such as the belief in 'white gods'. When the sixteenth-century Spanish conquistadores arrived in the Americas, they were greeted as gods, which facilitated the annihilation of the people who welcomed them. Apparently, the Incas mistook the Spanish invaders for Viracocha ('the white god') because of their lighter skin.[6]

We humans are storytellers. Animals may be familiar with objective realities outside of themselves (the natural world) as well as subjective experiences within themselves (e.g. fear and desire), but humans live in a triple-layered reality which contains narratives (stories) about the other two realities.[7] These stories are used to make sense of the world, and language plays a crucial part in them. Stories are the fabric of our lives, the building blocks of religions as well as economic and other systems. Typically, these stories are incompatible. Thus, one cannot adhere to Islam and Christianity at the same time, or be a capitalist and a communist. Such narratives are laid down in texts (the Koran, the Bible, *The Wealth of Nations*, *The Communist Manifesto*) and disseminated by institutions (churches, schools, organizations, governments). As the narratives are mutually exclusive (e.g. 'Christians are infidels', 'the Pope is infallible', 'religion is the opium of the people', 'it's the economy, stupid'), they lead to conflicts and even wars. Again, language plays a crucial role in these wars. In *Animal Farm*, George Orwell parodied the sloganesque language commonly used in narratives. His Seventh Commandment, for example, first reads, 'All animals are equal', while the crucial part 'but some animals are more equal than others' is later added.[8] The commandment eventually becomes the only remaining commandment and is used to justify the pigs' rule over the farm. Orwell is mocking Soviet socialism, but his parody applies to any story-producing system, or *ideology*. Thus, socialism and communism are ideologies, as are nationalism, capitalism, Christianity, Islam, humanism, ecology, and so on.

Ideology is a tricky word. It can mean entirely different things depending on who is using it.[9] Generally speaking, an ideology refers to the assumptions, beliefs, or ideas held by a group of people, and to the narratives they construct to support their ideas. Thus, an ideology can be defined as stories shared by particular groups in a society.[10] They typically develop into a set of comprehensive and consistent ideas that are used not only to make sense of the world, but also to change it (that is, to make the world better). This broad definition applies to political ideologies such as Marxism or liberalism as well as to religious beliefs such as Christianity and Islam. These ideologies are explicit, as the beliefs they rely on are laid down in texts which are regarded as their foundation stones (e.g. *Das Kapital* for Marxism, the Bible for Christianity). Moreover, they are institutionalized, and large groups of people accept their teachings as valid.

Yet ideologies can also be implicit, in which case they are much more difficult to define. This is often the case with language ideologies – the beliefs underlying actual language behaviour or language policies. These beliefs do not constitute an explicit, comprehensive, consistent set of ideas, but rather an implicit series of assumptions, which may be referred to as a 'cluster of beliefs' in one's mind.[11] Language ideologies may be linked to explicit ideologies such as Marxism, but they can also exist across different ideologies. For instance, the belief that language is the essence of one's identity is commonly held by nationalists, but it may be present in other ideologies as well, albeit in a more diluted form. The prevailing language ideologies in today's world have largely been influenced by three movements originating in three European traditions: French Rationalism, German Romanticism, and what may be labelled Anglo-Saxon Pragmatism. I discuss each of these ideologies briefly in the paragraphs that follow.

According to the French Enlightenment ideal, a nation is a contract between people, meaning that one's ethnic language, culture, and identity are not essential, and subordinated to 'Frenchness'. A nation, in other words, is an artificial arrangement for organizing society in an efficient way. The French insistence on linguistic uniformity implied that French was to be used in all areas ruled by France, and this policy was implemented ruthlessly in all French territories. As a result, local languages were suppressed, and French was the only language used by the government, administration, media, and so on. In education, too, French was the only language permitted. This explains why in today's France and in its overseas territories, the French language is disseminated in virtually all domains of society.

French was regarded as the universal language, superior to all other languages. A good example of this language ideology is provided by the French writer Antoine de Rivarol, who published an essay in 1784 with the self-explanatory title *Discours sur l'universalité de la langue française* (in English: *The Universality of the French Language*).[12] In his essay, the author stresses the intrinsic values of France and the French language, which he claims is the only language in which ideas can be expressed so clearly. According to Rivarol, the other major European languages are inferior to French when it comes to grammar and pronunciation. German is also condemned for its Gothic writing system, which he regards as shocking. Perhaps his harshest criticism is reserved for England, which he describes as a country isolated from the rest of the world. As Rivarol sees it, French deserves to be the universal language and he cannot imagine this position being threatened by any other language. With hindsight, these ideas may seem very naïve, but they had a major impact at the time they were written.

The linkage between ethnic language and identity is in large part a product of German Romanticism, itself a reaction to the rationalism of the Enlightenment and a rejection of French cultural dominance. The political nationalism of the French Revolution contrasts sharply with German linguistic nationalism. The ideology which 'essentializes' the links between language and ethnic identity is called *essentialism*. It was the German Romantics Herder, Fichte, and Humboldt who were the main advocates of an 'organic' nationalism in which language and culture were viewed as central to the character (*Volksgeist*) of the nation. Wilhelm von Humboldt, the linguist, and his younger brother Alexander, the naturalist, held similar ideas concerning language and nature. Although largely forgotten in the English-speaking world, Alexander von Humboldt was a precursor of Darwin's evolutionary theory and he was also an ecologist *avant la lettre*. He saw nature as an interconnected whole, an idea which was entirely new at that time. Much in the same way, Wilhelm von Humboldt saw language as a living organism which had to be understood in its wider context, involving landscape, culture, and people.[13] It was only much later that these ideas regarding organic ethnicity were discredited and perverted by nationalism, especially during the Nazi era.

The difference between the French and German views on language can be traced back to the conceptualization of the German *Kulturnation* and the French *Staatsnation*. A *Kulturnation* (literally a 'cultural nation') is a community of people with a common culture that finds its expression in, for instance, an ethnic language, tradition, or history. This German idea of a *Kulturnation* contrasts with the French idea of a *Staatsnation* (a nation-state), in which a nation is a mere contract among its people. The emergence of these two different views is rooted in history: Germany was unified as late as 1871, when the nation became a nation-state, whereas France had been a unified state for centuries. Even today, Germany has a federal state structure which reflects the differences between its *Länder*, whereas France is the example par excellence of a centralized state.

The policies applied by England, the dominant power in the British Isles, towards the ethnic languages used in Ireland, Wales, and Scotland were very similar to the French policies, but there is a striking difference between what may be called the French 'institutionalized' language policy and the Anglo-Saxon 'privatized' policy. The French policy is embodied by institutions such as the *Académie française*, the official authority on the usage, vocabulary, and grammar of the French language. The Academy publishes the official dictionary of the French language and decides on issues such as the use of English terms in the French media, which it vehemently opposes (rather unsuccessfully, though, as English words are widely used in France these days). Established in 1635, the French Academy consists of 40 members, known as *les immortels* (the immortals) as they hold office for life (most of its members are old, white, and male). The very concept of a language academy is unknown in the English-speaking world, and often leads to incomprehension. As Steven Pinker put it, the purpose of the French Academy is to 'amuse journalists from other countries with bitterly argued decisions that the French gaily ignore'.[14] Unlike France, English-speaking countries do not have centralized language policies, and thus there is no English Language Academy. Anglo-Saxon countries appear to prefer privatized language policies (removed from government control), based on liberal laissez-faire practices, perhaps reflecting the way Anglo-Saxon societies are organized. Moreover, the French normative tradition (i.e. the stress on 'standard' usage and the doctrine of linguistic correctness) contrasts sharply with the Anglo-Saxon aversion to 'linguistic engineering',[15] or deliberate efforts to prescribe how language should be used. Whereas Francophones generally have an explicit allegiance to their language, this is less the case with Anglophones, who do not often feel a close affinity towards their language.[16]

To sum up, in nineteenth-century Europe, the then Great Powers – and France in particular – imposed their language and culture on their territories as part of a process of nation- and state-building. In this way, the communities were imagined, to put it in Anderson's terms. While the dominant languages became all-pervasive in government, education, the army, and so on, the minority languages were pushed aside and their speakers were discriminated against, put in prison, and even killed. As a reaction, a new kind of nationalism surged in the nineteenth century, standing up for the rights of suppressed languages and cultures. This *language struggle* could be observed all over Europe: in Ireland, Norway, Finland, and Flanders, to mention just a few. New identities were imagined in which ethnic languages played a crucial role. Even today, we see that in various regions all over the world, very strong bonds have been established between language and identity, and that language is often a driving force in the process of nation-building or the maintenance of the nation-state.

Imagining new communities

In today's societies, the picture has become more complex. Groups of people are imagining new communities based on linguistic and – increasingly – religious identities. These new identities clash with established identities and reveal the fault lines of our modern societies. Even though the names of many European states refer to those states' dominant groups and their languages (as in England, Germany, and France), the old paradigm of 'one state, one language' no longer holds. Even France, which once took great pride in its Frenchness, is no longer the 'French' state it used to be. The same applies to virtually all other countries whose names refer to their national languages.

Communities are imagined not only from within, but also from outside. As a result, a name adopted by an imagined community may not please another imagined community. Since Yugoslavia broke apart and the Republic of Macedonia came into being in 1991, the country has lacked an official, internationally agreed name because of Greece's objections to the name Macedonia. In 2019, the two countries agreed on the name North Macedonia. This name change led to violent protests and a government crisis in Greece, however. According to Greece, the name Macedonia belongs to them because of historical, territorial, and ethnic reasons. In their view, Macedonia is the northern region in Greece, where Greeks identify themselves as Macedonians, though these Macedonians are not to be confused with the Slavic people living on the other side of the border. Furthermore, the new republic was accused of appropriating symbols that are essentially Greek (such as the Vergina Sun, the rayed solar symbol featuring in ancient Greek art). As a result of the ongoing dispute with Greece, Macedonia became a member of the United Nations under the provisional name Former Yugoslav Republic of Macedonia (FYROM). As a word, the acronym FYROM is devoid of meaning, but it sounded harmless and therefore it was acceptable to all parties concerned.

There may be some irony in the fact that today, ethnic minority languages in Europe are actually being supported by their former oppressors (that is, the nation-states), and action has been taken to revive them. The Council of Europe even signed a Charter for Regional and Minority Languages in recognition of their cultural value.[17] Unfortunately, for many of these languages, official recognition may come too late, as many have become extinct after years of oppression. On the Isle of Man, for instance, efforts are being made to revive Manx, also known as Manx Gaelic. Even though Manx is considered an important part of the island's heritage, only a small minority of the population is fluent in the language. The same may be said of Irish, which is the first official language of the Irish Republic, despite the fact that the vast majority of Irish people are monolingual speakers of English. Other languages have fared better, such as Catalan, which has been successfully institutionalized as an official language in Catalonia since the beginning of Spain's transition to democracy in 1975. As Catalonia had been at the centre of resistance against the Franco regime since the 1930s, the suppression of Catalan by the Spanish government had a clear political motivation.

Apart from ethnic minority languages, contemporary Europe hosts a myriad of other languages, many originating outside the continent. These include the languages spoken by migrants who arrived from the former colonies from the 1940s onwards, so-called guest workers from countries such as Turkey and Morocco beginning in the 1960s, and recent waves of new immigrants from Syria and other war-torn countries. This influx of people has led to unparalleled cultural and linguistic complexity, and to the construction of new identities. Many people speak different languages or language varieties in different situations, and languages are being mixed, changed, and adopted. In this age of increasing diversity (often referred to as *superdiversity*), existing imagined communities are being challenged and new imagined communities are emerging. In the major cities all over Europe, one can hear young people, often of mixed descent, say something in one language, then switch to another language – known as code-switching – before addressing someone else in a third or even fourth language.

In spite of these multilingual practices, which remind us of the Tower of Babel, one language has emerged as the global lingua franca, a language that is used as a common language by speakers of different languages. This language is English. Yet English may not be the common language it is often supposed to be, as there are many varieties of English and not everyone has equal access to it. In many parts of the world, it is not English, but some other language, which serves as the lingua franca. This is a complex topic, and one which is explored in more detail in Chapter 6.

Imagined communities may be groups of people with particular needs who use language to serve particular purposes, such as deaf people (sign language) and blind people (Braille, for reading purposes). Families (children and/or their parents), communities based on gender or race, and even secret groups (e.g. gangs) may also have their own languages. These languages are not necessarily 'complete' languages, but they enable communication with insiders while warding off outsiders. Thus, a particular bond or identity may be established. For instance, when homosexuality was still illegal in the United Kingdom, Polari was used as a form of gay slang. Although there is very little agreement about the spelling, pronunciation, and meaning of words, Polari made it possible to communicate in public without risking arrest. More fundamentally, the secret language both concealed and revealed one's identity simultaneously.[18] An example of Polari would be something like *palone vadas omi-palone very cod*, which means 'that woman is giving me dirty looks'. In order to reveal their sexual identity, speakers would drop a word or two of Polari into conversation with a new acquaintance as a kind of password. If the other person was also gay, they could respond accordingly. In the late 1960s and early 1970s, people who dressed flamboyantly and would have been identified as gay would use Polari in quite an aggressive way to respond to stares or remarks from members of the public. It was a way of confounding and confusing the public, who would have known they were being insulted without being able to understand what exactly was being said.[19]

Race can also serve as a marker of one's linguistic identity. Palenque de San Basilio is a small village in northern Colombia, which I visited in 2017. Its 3,500 inhabitants are descendants of African slaves who managed to escape and set up a community where they could live in freedom. Palenque, which literally means 'walled city', is considered the first free town on the American continent. Its language, Palenquero (also known as Palenque), is strongly influenced by Kongo, one of the Bantu languages spoken in Congo and Angola. In spite of the claim that Palenquero is a *living* language (*lengua ri Palenge a ten mbila*, as the slogan reads),[20] it is in fact moribund, as most of its speakers are old people.[21] Nowadays, young people are learning it as a second language and as a marker of their imagined community, which is alive and kicking. In the local school – basically a couple of barracks around a small courtyard – children are no longer taught only in Spanish, but also in their heritage language. The question remains, however, whether this will be enough to save the language from extinction. The slogan 'black is beautiful', which is written on one of the walls in Palenque, is interesting in itself. It is one of the few signs in English in the entire village where hardly anyone speaks English. Interestingly, in the northern United States in the early 1960s, the word 'black' was an offensive term which later in the decade became to be embraced.[22]

The language or way of speaking used in an imagined community may also be adopted by individuals who aspire to belong to that particular group or social class. This is perhaps most noticeable in accents. Some people do this professionally, such as actors. The American actress Meryl Streep is particularly well known for her accent adaptation, including a Danish accent in *Out of Africa* (a film in which she played Danish author Karen Blixen), an Italian accent in *The Bridges of Madison County*, and British RP (received pronunciation, or 'BBC English') in *The French Lieutenant's Woman* and *The Iron Lady*. In the latter film, she played Margaret

FIGURE 3.2 Palenque de San Basilio
Source: Frank van Splunder

Thatcher. Interestingly, the accent put on by Streep in this film had in fact been put on by Thatcher herself. The former British prime minister deliberately shifted away from her native Lincolnshire accent towards RP to signify a higher social class.[23] Another former British PM, Tony Blair, did almost the opposite, moving from a posh RP some way towards Cockney, the accent traditionally spoken by working-class Londoners. Whereas Margaret Thatcher was attempting to show solidarity with her Conservative voters, Tony Blair was doing the same with his Labour audience.[24]

New circumstances may demand a different language altogether, not just a different accent. In *The History of Love*, a contemporary novel written by Nicole Krauss, the protagonists are two old men – both of them survivors of the Holocaust and émigrés to the United States – who prefer to speak English instead of Yiddish, the language of their youth and a reminder of a painful past. One of them remarks, 'we never speak in Yiddish. The words of our childhood became strangers to us – we couldn't use them in the same way and so we chose not to use them at all. Life demanded a new language.'[25] This new language is English, the language of their adopted country. Sadly enough, the old men's imagined community is a relic of the past, a world which no longer exists.

To sum up this chapter: people and groups of people, both small or large, use particular languages, language varieties, and linguistic features such as accents to confirm their belonging to particular imagined communities and to reject or hide other identities. However, identities are also established by others, who may judge (and even condemn) one's language or accent. Tiny differences can be of tremendous importance. A person who speaks with a slightly different accent will be marked as an outsider, for instance. This happens to people from neighbouring villages and to non-native speakers of a language, even if they speak their second language very fluently. An accent, however slight, can serve to mark someone out as a 'foreigner' even after they have lived somewhere for many years and long after they have stopped regarding themselves as such.

Notes

1 Anderson (1983: 6).
2 The Kurdish Institute of Paris, the organization which deals with Kurdish language, culture, and history, estimates the Kurds to number between 30 and 45 million (2017 estimate). See: www.institutkurde.org/en/ (accessed 7 October 2019).
3 Anthony D. Smith (1991: 14) defines a nation as 'a named human population sharing an historic territory, common myths and historical memories, a mass, public culture, a common economy and common legal rights and duties for all members'.
4 Gellner (1983).
5 Gat and Yakobson (2013).
6 Mills and Taylor (1988: 39).
7 Harari (2017: 81).
8 Orwell (1945).
9 McLean and McMillan (2003: 256–257).

10 Stibbe (2015).
11 Van Dijk (1998).
12 de Rivarol (1784, 1995).
13 Wulf (2015: 199). Although largely forgotten in the Anglo-Saxon world, Alexander von Humboldt's name is everywhere in Latin America, where he travelled widely. The name Humboldt graces many national parks, rivers, mountains, animals, and plant species, as well as scientific institutions.
14 Pinker (1994: 370).
15 Haugen (1987).
16 Shell (2002).
17 See:www.coe.int/en/web/conventions/full-list/-/conventions/rms/0900001680695175 (accessed 7 October 2019).
18 Baker (2004).
19 Paul Baker, personal communication, 4 March 2019. Contemporary examples of how language can be used to express gay identity can be found at http://rupaulsdragrace.fandom.com/wiki/RuPaul%27s_Drag_Race_Dictionary (accessed 6 March 2019).
20 See: www.youtube.com/watch?v=S6KPnfr1IYQ (accessed 20 March 2019).
21 See: www.ethnologue.com (accessed 18 March 2018).
22 Joseph (2006: 97).
23 Moreover, in the earlier years of her career, Thatcher adopted a deeper tone to sound more commanding.
24 Why people change the way they speak: www.youtube.com/watch?v=uf0DDm9NYcI (accessed 20 March 2018).
25 Krauss (2005: 6).

4
LANGUAGE AS A CONSTRUCTION

A dialect with an army

So far, I have discussed the pervasive power of language, the origins and nature of language, and the way language is used to imagine a particular community. I have not yet defined what exactly constitutes a language, or what (if anything) makes it different from a dialect. The focus of this chapter is on languages and dialects (or language varieties, as I will call them) and how these varieties change over time and from place to place. We will also look at how language is constructed in writing (script, spelling), word choice (vocabulary), and structure (grammar).

At first sight, the terms language and dialect appear to be clear-cut concepts. In reality, however, they are far more complex than we could ever imagine. First of all, the difference between a language and a dialect is often based on political or ideological factors rather than linguistic criteria. It has therefore been argued that a language is a 'dialect with an army', a phrase attributed to the linguist Max Weinreich.[1] In Yiddish, the phrase reads *a shprakh iz a dyalekt mit an armey un flot* (a language is a dialect with an army and navy). What this means is that any language comes in different varieties, and that the most powerful variety – the one with the army – is called a language, whereas the other varieties are called dialects.

The power of a language variety is determined by its speakers' dominance in political, economic, social, and cultural domains. The variety used by the dominant group will be codified in dictionaries and grammars, and imposed as the standard for all speakers. With the help of this 'army', the variety will be disseminated in education and in all other domains of society, as a result of which it gains even more prestige. The other varieties (the dialects) are not usually codified, not taught in formal education, and lack prestige. As power shifts over time, varieties may gain or lose prestige. Afrikaans, for instance, was long considered a dialect of Dutch, for which the derogatory term 'kitchen language' (*kombuistaal*) was used. In the early twentieth century, however, Afrikaans began to develop into a distinct, standardized language. Though long identified with Afrikaner white nationalism and the apartheid system, today Afrikaans is one of the 11 official languages of South Africa and the majority of its speakers are not white at all.

Most people tend to think of languages as clearly distinct entities. This is also suggested by their names, which often refer to particular countries or people. Thus, English and German are clearly different languages, and so are the countries where these languages are spoken and the people who speak them. This, however, is the surface level. English and German are in fact closely related, as both of them belong to the same branch of West Germanic languages, to which Dutch, Frisian, Afrikaans, and Yiddish also belong. If you go far back enough in history, it is actually very difficult to tell them apart, as the following example illustrates.

In 1932, the following sentence was discovered on the flyleaf of a manuscript kept in Oxford: *Hebban olla vogala nestas hagunnan hinase hic anda thu, wat unbidan we nu?* In modern English, it means: All birds have started making nests, except you and me, what are we waiting for? The sentence can easily be interpreted as a love poem, even though the meaning is not entirely clear. The sentence was probably written around 1100 by the monk who was copying Latin and Old English texts into the manuscript. From time to time, he would have had to sharpen the goose quill he was using for copying the texts. Perhaps he wrote the sentence on the last page to test his newly sharpened quill. Based on linguistic analysis, the sentence was identified as Dutch rather than English and became famous as the first sentence ever to be written in Dutch. Nowadays, following its marketization, the sentence features on many T-shirts and postcards in the Netherlands and Flanders. *Olla vogala* was probably written by a Flemish monk who was living and working in an English monastery, and who wrote the sentence in his local variety of Old Dutch. Yet more recent research has suggested that the sentence may not be Dutch after all, but English (that is, the Kent dialect of Old English).[2] For today's speakers of English or Dutch, however, the sentence is barely recognizable as one of these languages, and it appears to be a foreign language. The example shows just how much languages change over time and how they develop indeed into 'foreign' languages. Similar examples may be found in other languages all over the world.

The languages we speak today derive from languages we can no longer understand, and future generations will find it very difficult to understand us. However, there is no clear linguistic break between these languages, as the changes occur very gradually. Moreover, languages not only change over time, but also from place to place. That is, a language slowly develops into another language, while both languages still exist. Take the example of German and Dutch, two languages which are even more closely related than English and German. Even though their standard varieties are clearly distinct, their dialects slowly develop from German into Dutch, and the other way round. From a linguistic point of view, some of the dialects spoken in the Netherlands have more in common with German than with Dutch. For example, the German pronoun *ich* (meaning I) is used in the dialects spoken in the south-eastern part of the Netherlands and Flanders, though the standard pronoun in Dutch is *ik*, which is also used in the north of Germany where Low German (*Plattdeutsch*) is spoken. Similar overlaps can be observed in other areas where closely related languages are spoken, such as in the Scandinavian language area. Like German and Dutch – or Dutch and Afrikaans – Danish, Norwegian, and Swedish are mutually intelligible (depending on which area a speaker comes from), but they are called different languages because of political and cultural realities. On the other hand, speakers of *Schwyzerdütsch* (the German spoken in Switzerland) are very difficult to understand for other speakers of German. We may say that these languages reflect imagined communities in that they refer to the nations they helped to establish.

According to Heinz Kloss, a German linguist (and former member of the Nazi Party),[3] there are two criteria for a dialect to be recognized as a language. He made a distinction between *Abstand* ('distance') and *Ausbau* ('building out'),[4] which is still relevant today. *Abstand* means that a dialect must be sufficiently distinct from a recognized language, while *Ausbau* means that it must be sufficiently elaborated (e.g. with a standardized spelling or grammar). The model explains why English and German, for instance, are considered related but separate languages, while Chinese is considered one language, even though many of its variants are not mutually understandable. In Kloss's terms: the *Abstand* between some variants of Chinese is as significant as the one between English and German, but the *Ausbau* is much smaller (due to the fact that the Chinese are an imagined community, while England and Germany are not). The Arabic-speaking world is similar to the Chinese imagined community in this respect – which will be discussed in the next chapter.

Naming and shaming

Borders between languages tend to be artificial, and languages themselves are not as natural as they are often perceived to be either. As discussed in the previous chapter, language can play a crucial role in the construction of a nation or a nation-state. In Europe, languages are generally separated from each other clearly, at least as far as the standard varieties are concerned. As observed earlier, this is often reflected in the names of these languages, which establish clear links between the language, its territory, and people (as in the country names France or England). This is not always possible, however, as a country can have more than one language (e.g. Belgium, Switzerland), and one language can be spoken in more than one country (e.g. English, French, German). On other continents, there appear to be considerably more languages than in Europe, and the division between language and dialect tends to be less clear-cut. The reason is that European perceptions of languages reflect ideas about the nation-state, ideas which developed in a nineteenth-century European context.

Languages themselves are also constructed. This holds not only for languages such as Esperanto, which have been devised to serve a particular purpose, but also for so-called natural languages such as English, French, and Spanish. Rules are made to codify a language, but also to make it different from another variety or, alternatively, to make it more similar. These rules can apply to the spelling, grammar, or vocabulary of a language, and as the rules make it into dictionaries and grammars, the differences (or similarities) are disseminated in the education system. It is important to note that such rules reflect political decisions, often implemented top-down by a governing body or a language academy, such as the *Académie française* or the *Real Academia de la Lengua Española*.

A good example of language policy that aimed to codify differences rather than similarities can be found in former Yugoslavia. While after the Second World War Yugoslavia was united around Tito and the communist bureaucracy, after the break-up of the country between 1992 and 2006 the newly emerging states wanted to emphasize their differences. The name Serbo-Croatian as a cover term for the languages used in Yugoslavia fell into disuse and was replaced by the names Bosnian, Croatian, Serbian, and Montenegrin, reflecting the new states. The varieties were actually made different from each other, as separate standards were codified and implemented. As a result, separate linguistic identities were created, serving political purposes. The languages also *look* different, as they use different alphabets. While today's Croatian and Bosnian make use of the Latin alphabet only, Serbian uses both (the Cyrillic alphabet is dominant – including its use in religion – but the Latin alphabet is used for commercial purposes). The use of two alphabets can be confusing as, for instance, road signs to CAPAJEBO (in Cyrillic) and others to SARAJEVO (in Latin) in fact refer to the same city.[5] From a linguistic point of view, however, the languages spoken in former Yugoslavia may be regarded as one *pluricentric* language consisting of mutually intelligible standard varieties, as may be observed in other languages as well (e.g. in English, German, French, Spanish). In Kloss's terms, the *Abstand* between the varieties is very small, while their *Ausbau* is a work in progress.

Alternatively, language policy can also aim to stress the similarities between varieties rather than their differences. This tendency could be observed in Flanders, the northern part of Belgium, a country characterized by linguistic tensions between the north and its French-speaking neighbours in the south. The official name of the language spoken in Flanders is Dutch and not Flemish. The use of the term Flemish instead of Dutch is misleading, as it suggests that they are different languages. This can be useful, of course: the name Flemish was used deliberately when Belgium was created as an independent state in 1830 to differentiate it from the Netherlands.[6] The later decision to call the language Dutch was also political, as it stressed the close linguistic ties between Flanders and the Netherlands. They work together in the Dutch Language Union, an intergovernmental organization which was set up to discuss language policy issues in the Low Countries. Similar organizations exist in other parts of the world as well, for instance the *Organisation internationale de la Francophonie* (OIF, generally known as *la Francophonie*), which represents countries where a significant proportion of the population are speakers of French. Interestingly, there is no equivalent for this organization in the English-speaking world. The Commonwealth, which comprises mostly former territories of the British Empire, may be similar in scope or structure, but essentially deals with issues related to politics and economics rather than language.

40 Language is politics

The names given to places can also be highly political, of course, and the names of streets and cities can be changed to serve a particular ideology. For instance, during the Second World War, the Nazis banned all street names which referred to Jews. When the communists came to power after the war, they even changed the names of whole cities. Thus, the German city of Chemnitz in the former German Democratic Republic (an interesting name in itself) was called Karl-Marx-Stadt between 1953 and 1990, and reverted to its old name after the collapse of the GDR. New names are not always accepted easily. Mumbai, one of the major cities on India's west coast, is often still called Bombay, the old colonial name.[7] People sometimes change their own names to express allegiance to a particular community. Emigrants who adopt the language of their new country may change their names too. For example, in order to blend in in his newly adopted country, the United States, French-speaking Jean-Pierre chose to call himself John instead (while for his family in Europe, he remained Jean-Pierre). Sometimes people are forced to change their names or are given derogatory names. This can also happen to entire communities (e.g. 'Bushmen' for the Khoisan people in southern Africa). After all, there is more in a name than we may be aware of.

Constructing languages

Spelling wars

The most visible aspect of a language is the way it is written. If the spelling or alphabet of a language changes, it looks very different (though it remains the same language, with the same vocabulary and grammar). When the United States gained independence in 1776, they wanted to demonstrate both their political and linguistic independence from their former colonizers. It was therefore suggested that their language be referred to as *American* rather than English. The most visible differences between the two varieties are in the spelling of what is now called British and American English. Noah Webster, the author of *An American Dictionary of the English Language*, was not only a lexicographer and a spelling reformer, but also a man with a political mission. Webster believed that the American nation was superior to Europe, a superiority he wanted to reveal in the new nation's language. As a spelling reformer, he preferred spellings that matched pronunciation and that could be taught easily. As a result, centre became center, and programme was shortened to program. Other spelling changes included labour (AE labor), dialogue (AE dialog), aesthetic (AE esthetic), traveller (AE traveler) and analyse (AE analyze). Although 'programme' is the preferred spelling in British English, 'program' is often used in computing contexts (e.g. computer program), which reflects the global dominance of American English.

The spelling of English remains notoriously complex. The Irish writer G.B. Shaw highlighted its wackiness when he suggested that the word 'fish' could be spelled 'ghoti': *gh* as in tou*gh*, *o* as in w*o*men and *ti* as in na*ti*on. In many other language areas, spelling and spelling reforms have led to emotional debates, as spelling is something people feel very strongly about (more than grammar, for instance, which is less visible). In the Dutch language area, the spelling reform that took place after the Second World War revealed a split between the Netherlands and Flanders. Whereas Flanders preferred the use of k over c in certain loan words (e.g. in the word democracy, from Greek δημοκρατία), in the Netherlands it was the other way round. The reason is political: the c appeared more French, which was difficult to accept for the Flemings, whereas the k looked more German, which was difficult to accept for the Dutch. It was not until 1995 that the issue was settled in favour of the Dutch.

In Belgium, even the spelling of place names can be political. The place Schaarbeek (Dutch spelling) near Brussels is written Schaerbeek in French, reflecting the old Dutch spelling with -ae instead of -aa. The new Dutch spelling has never been adopted by the French-speaking community. On official signs, the place is referred to as Schaarbeek/Schaerbeek. The two spellings look almost identical, but reveal a world of differences. Some other places have entirely different names, such as Mons, which is called Bergen in Dutch (the literal translation of Mons, which means mountains). For tourists visiting Belgium, this can be pretty frustrating, as the two sides of the linguistic border use their own versions of the place names. A road sign to Ghent reads *Gent* in Dutch-speaking Flanders, but *Gand* in French-speaking Wallonia. On a road sign in the Brussels area which said 'Luxembourg', the o had to be removed as the sign was situated in Dutch-speaking territory, where the spelling is *Luxemburg*. The empty space between the b and the u was left clearly visible on the road sign.

Another example from South America shows how the (mis)spelling of a country's name can cause considerable controversy. The country Colombia (with an o in the second syllable) is often spelled Columbia (with a u) in English. The mistake is understandable, as North America has several Columbias, including Columbia University in New York and the Canadian province of British Columbia, which are all written with a u. Yet the inhabitants of Colombia take offence when the name of their country is not written with an o. A campaign was even launched to eradicate the persistent spelling mistake. Although the campaign appeared to be very successful from a commercial point of view (the mistake was skilfully merchandised), it did not manage to suppress the spelling mistake. Interestingly, both Colombia and Columbia derive from the same source: the name of the explorer who 'discovered' the Americas in 1492 and who opened up the New World for conquest by Europeans. However, in Spanish his name is Cristóbal Colón (hence Colombia), while in English he is known as Christopher Columbus (hence Columbia). The spelling confusion is thus rooted in the continent's colonial history.

Other countries have had their spelling wars too. These wars are often fought between language academies and language users, especially teachers and journalists. As the 1996 German spelling reform (*Rechtschreibereform*) was opposed by a majority of teachers, writers, and newspapers, a spelling war ensued, and eventually a heavily watered-down version of the reform was implemented. The French spelling reform introduced by the *Académie française* in 2016 (basically a simplified orthography regarding the use of the circumflex) caused widespread outrage, as it was seen as

42 Language is politics

FIGURE 4.1 Colombia merchandising
Source: Frank van Splunder

an attack on the French language. The controversy also highlighted fears about 'English taking over' in France, and the use of English loan words in particular. Some languages change the spelling of foreign words and even names of people into their own orthography, as a result of which the original language may barely be recognizable. Very few readers are likely to recognize Xhorxh Oruelli, unless you tell them that this is the Albanian spelling of George Orwell.

Changing the writing system of a language is even more drastic than just changing the spelling. Yet this has happened too, for instance in Turkish and Vietnamese, both of which have adopted the Latin alphabet. The main advantage of the Latin alphabet is its simplicity compared to the Arabic and Chinese writing systems, as a result of which it can be learnt relatively easily. Apart from this functional advantage, a language written in the Latin alphabet looks more Western, or less 'traditional'. This consideration was indeed a crucial element of the Turkish 'alphabet revolution' (*harf devrimi*), which took place in 1928. After the fall of the Ottoman Empire, the new Turkish Republic wanted to look westwards instead of eastwards, as a consequence of which the Arabic script was replaced by the Latin alphabet. This language policy was instigated by Mustafa Kemal Atatürk, the 'father' of the modern Turkish nation, whose aim was to westernize and modernize the country. Language reform was an important part of Atatürk's nationalist programme. The aim of the Turkish 'language revolution' (*dil devrimi*) was to create a language that was more specifically Turkish and less Arabic, Persian, and Islamic. In addition, Atatürk wanted a language that was modern and easier to learn. Apart from the adoption of a new alphabet, the other main strategy consisted of 'purifying' the vocabulary. Arabic and Persian words were dropped from dictionaries and replaced by resurrected archaic words or words from Turkish dialects. By introducing these changes in the language, Turkey turned consciously towards the West and severed the links with its Islamic heritage. At the same time, many words were adopted from French, which was then the international language of prestige. These words were adapted to the Turkish spelling, so that they look Turkish rather than French at first sight. A good example is the word *afiş*, which derives from the French *affiche* (banner or poster). Other examples are *asansör* (French *ascenseur*, English: lift), *kuaför* (French *coiffeur*, English: hairdresser), and *şömine* (French *cheminée*, English: fireplace). It has been argued that in undergoing this language revolution, Turkey estranged itself from the linguistic and literary heritage of the Ottomans. Yet it should be noted that this argument is politically loaded and commonly associated with the 'neo-Ottomanist' sentiments of the current regime in Turkey. Although the regime appears to be looking more eastwards than westwards, and many Islamic terms have been introduced since the emergence of Islamism in the 1990s, Turkey will not go back to its Arabic writing system.

In Vietnam, the Latin script was introduced by Portuguese missionaries in the sixteenth century for teaching and evangelization purposes. The traditional Vietnamese writing system, which was based on Chinese characters, was abolished by the emperor in 1918, and by the 1930s the Latin script had become the dominant writing system. The main advantage of the new Vietnamese alphabet was that it facilitated widespread literacy among Vietnamese speakers. As in Turkey, it has been argued that the introduction of the Latin alphabet cut Vietnam off from its traditional literature and culture. Unlike Vietnam, the People's Republic of China, which was established in 1949, did not abolish its characters. Yet they were simplified, reflecting Mao Zedong's communist language ideology: mass literacy could only be achieved by using simplified characters. Currently, traditional Chinese characters are being used in Taiwan, Hong Kong, Macau, and in Chinese communities within and outside South East Asia. In conclusion, the abolition of a traditional script or characters and the adoption of a new script, or simplified characters, can have far-reaching consequences, perhaps unforeseen by language planners and changers, whose main purpose is ideological or educational.

Grammar and vocabulary

Other changes in a language may be less visible than the alphabet or spelling, but their impact should not be underestimated. Grammar and vocabulary can serve political purposes too. Personal pronouns are a good example. Whereas modern English has only one second-person personal pronoun (*you*), many languages have a system of two or more pronouns to refer to their interlocutor's status (e.g. informal *du* and formal *Sie* in German, which are like *thou* and *you* in archaic English).

The choice between the two forms, which is informed by social conventions, has grammatical consequences. Thus, 'you can' translates as either *du kannst* or *Sie können* in German. Moreover, the switch between *du* and *Sie* (or *tu* and *vous* in French) will have considerable interpersonal consequences (e.g. intimacy or distance can be created). Many non-Western languages such as Arabic or Javanese (a language spoken in Indonesia) use far more complicated systems to express 'you'. In Japanese, which has a much broader vocabulary for saying 'you', there is a strong tendency not to use the Japanese word for 'you' (*anata*) at all, as it may sound impolite. It is considered more polite to use a person's name instead.

On a more political level, the use of a particular personal pronoun can be linked to the class struggle. The leaders of the French Revolution, for instance, forbade the use of the deferential form *vous* along with titles. In their efforts to create a classless society, the leaders of the Russian Revolution pursued similar policies.[8] In Cuban Spanish, informal *tú* is used more often than in Spain, which often uses *usted* instead. During the 1959 Cuban Revolution, the word *compañero* (*compañera* for women) was introduced to replace *señor* (*señora*) as the latter was thought to stigmatize a person's social position. In contrast, the word *compañero(a)* was used to express equality and to do away with social class distinctions. For many years, *compañero(a)* was the common word to address people in political speeches as well as in everyday life. These days, however, there is a tendency to use *señor(a)* again,[9] a word which can be used to express politeness, but also a changing social reality. For instance, in private restaurants, which did not exist until a couple of years ago, the word *señor(a)* may sound more acceptable than *compañero(a)*.

Apart from signifying social class and interpersonal power relations, pronouns can be used to indicate gender. So-called neutral third-person pronouns can be used to promote gender equality or to obscure gender differences altogether. In English, as in many other languages, one word is used to refer to males (he) and another one is used for females (she). Traditionally, the male form was used as the 'neutral' form, as in the sentence 'A doctor has many patients. *He* should take care of *his* patients'. The acceptability of this sentence was taken for granted in a world in which most doctors were indeed male, but in today's English it is a different story. Instead, the terms 'he/she' and '(s)he' are used for generic references. As this usage sometimes looks rather clumsy, 'they' may be used instead, as in 'Someone lost their book'. Yet this may annoy language purists, who argue that 'they' should be used to refer to plural nouns only. In 2019, however, Merriam-Webster added 'they' as a singular and non-binary pronoun to its dictionary, arguing that 'they' can be used as a *pronoun of choice* for someone who does not want to identify as either male or female.[10] The use of a particular pronoun may be an indication of when the sentence was written, as the following examples reveal (the year of publication is shown in brackets):

- Like the scientist, the historian examines his data and formulates hypotheses. (1955)
- We are talking about what a person has learned in the process of becoming a member of society that makes him react to his social world. (1967)

- A person learns a language better when he wants to be a member of the group speaking that language. (1969)
- Man is regarded as the creator of his environment. (1979)
- You are planning an office party. You invite your boss, the clerk who works under you, and your good friend, a fellow employee. You request that each of your guests come unaccompanied by his wife. (1980)
- The principal concern is with an understanding of the way in which the individual creates, modifies, and interprets the world in which he or she finds himself or herself. (2005)
- The interviewee can only retain a certain amount of information in her/his short-term memory. (2005)
- The researcher will need to locate her discussions of validity within the research paradigm that is being used. (2005)
- The reader will have to draw their own conclusions. (2011)

As an increasing number of people identify as neither male nor female (or as both), language planners are trying to respond to this changing reality. At the University of Vermont, students can choose to be addressed using a range of pronouns: he, she, they, as well as 'ze' (a 'non-traditional' pronoun) and 'name only'.[11] Wikipedia lists 13 non-traditional pronouns in English,[12] but none of them have made it into dictionaries or grammar books yet.

Some Scandinavian languages have introduced entirely new and gender-neutral pronouns. *Hen* was added to the Swedish Academic Wordlist in 2015, setting off a debate in Norway as well. In Norwegian, *hin* was constructed to fill the gap between *hun* (she) and *han* (he). Later, *hin* was changed into *hen*, yet *hin/hen* is rarely used, except by limited interest groups (e.g. those who do not identify with binary gender categories). The new pronoun has not been embraced by society as a whole. This may be because the pronoun was constructed – top-down language planning often faces resistance from language users.[13] None of this means that these new words are not important, however. At the very least, they stimulate debate about sex/gender and identity. And at best, they help establish the identity of a group that was previously invisible, whose very existence was denied by the use of binary pronouns.

It's worth mentioning the use of the honorific term 'Ms' instead of 'Mrs' or 'Miss', which reveal a woman's marital status, here too. The use of the neutral 'Ms' was brought into mainstream use by Sheila Michaelis, an American feminist. Although she did not invent the term, she apparently began using it after she saw it in an address, thinking it was a typo. Thus, the term was rescued from obscurity, and today it is widely used in English-speaking countries. More recently, the honorific 'Mx' appeared on the Oxford Dictionaries website, where it was defined as 'a title used before a person's surname or full name by those who wish to avoid specifying their gender or by those who prefer not to identify themselves as male or female'.[14] Again, it remains to be seen whether this usage will catch on.

Attempts to deliberately change a language do not always work, and there appears to be some kind of natural resistance to rules prescribed by language academies or other language planners (including teachers and parents). For instance, it's not so easy to ban words. Words can be banned because people find them offensive and they can be replaced by euphemisms (literally words of 'good omen'). These euphemisms often refer to taboo topics in the areas of sex, death, or disability. The very word 'disability', for instance, can be replaced by 'special needs', even though there are people who find the latter term offensive: people who require special needs might be viewed more negatively than people with a disability. Basically, it all depends on interpretation and connotations a particular word or phrase may evoke.

The use of 'barbarisms' should be mentioned here too. As the word suggests, barbarism is the absence of culture – a barbarism is a word or expression which is badly formed according to the rules set by language regulators who decide what is correct usage and what is an error or a deviation from standard usage. Of course, the words *badly formed*, *correct*, *error*, *deviation*, and *standard* are politically loaded as they reflect the language ideologies of the educated elite, who often hold conservative views. Many barbarisms are regional words which are used in areas where less dominant varieties of a particular language are spoken. In Scottish secondary schools, *Scotticisms* (words or phrases characteristic of Scots, a language closely related to English) were classified as barbarisms until the middle of the previous century, which would be unthinkable today.[15] Also, standard usage is determined by the variety typically spoken by the urban elite.

Words derived from a foreign language are a special case. Both the *Académie française* and the *Real Academia de la Lengua Española* have waged wars against what they call the invasion of English, but neither have been successful. In Italy, the battle against English is led by the centre-left newspaper *La Repubblica*, which in 2016 ran a double page with the headline *In altre parole* ('In other words'), arguing that Italian should be purged of English words and replenished with Italian equivalents. Yet efforts to 'purify' languages in this way appear to be counterproductive, as the current use of English words in France, Spain, Italy, and many other countries shows. The role of English in today's world is so pervasive that it will be discussed in Chapter 6.

The examples provided in this chapter aim to show that language is not just a means of communication. It can also become a tool – or a weapon – in the hands of politicians, language academicians, lexicographers, grammarians, language teachers and testers, publishers, and other gatekeepers who set the rules of the game. As we have seen, languages are shaped to carry out political missions and language ideologies. This may be most obvious in the spelling or the script of a language, but other aspects, such as grammar and vocabulary, can also be manipulated.

Notes

1 Spolsky (2014).
2 De Grauwe (2004). This article is available in Dutch only.
3 Hutton (2001:178).
4 Kloss (1967).

5 Road signs to Sarajevo in the Latin alphabet can be seen in Bosnia-Herzegovina, whereas in the *Republika Srpska* (the Serb Republic within Bosnia-Herzegovina) the city's name is written in the Cyrillic alphabet.
6 Dalby (2002).
7 Sudjic (2017: 42).
8 Joseph (2006: 73).
9 See: www.cubadebate.cu/especiales/2017/12/15/que-paso-con-la-palabra-companero/#.XOVIUa2B3aY (accessed 22 May 2019).
10 See: www.merriam-webster.com/words-at-play/singular-nonbinary-they (accessed 7 October 2019).
11 See: www.uvm.edu/registrar/preferred-name-and-pronoun (accessed 7 November 2018).
12 See: https://en.wikipedia.org/wiki/Third-person_pronoun (accessed 7 November 2018).
13 See discussion on Duolingo: www.duolingo.com/comment/21764588/Does-Norwegian-have-an-equivalent-to-the-Swedish-gender-neutral-pronoun-hen (accessed 7 November 2018).
14 See: https://en.oxforddictionaries.com/definition/mx (accessed 7 November 2018).
15 Joseph (2006: 8).

5
THE PECKING ORDER OF LANGUAGES

World languages and other languages

No one can tell for sure how many languages there are in the world. A reliable source is *Ethnologue*,[1] an encyclopaedic reference work that lists all living languages. Updated annually, *Ethnologue* is published by SIL International,[2] a Christian organization based in the United States whose main purpose is to document languages for religious reasons, including the translation of the Bible into local languages. According to *Ethnologue*, there are currently more than 7,000 languages in the world. Most of these languages are spoken in Asia (2,303) and in Africa (2,140), preceding the Pacific (1,322) and the Americas (1,058). Europe comes last, with 'only' 288 languages. Whereas some languages are spoken by millions of people, almost a third of all languages have less than 1,000 speakers. Some languages are spoken by a handful of people only, and when the last speaker dies, the language dies too.

Europe has considerably less languages than the other continents, but they are the most standardized languages in the world. This results from the process of nation-building in the continent, which began some 500 years ago and which culminated

TABLE 5.1 Languages in the world (*Ethnologue*, 2019)[3]

Continent	Languages	Percentage
Asia	2,303	32%
Africa	2,140	30%
Pacific	1,322	19%
Americas	1,058	15%
Europe	288	4%
TOTAL	7,111	100 %

in the emergence of the nation-state in the nineteenth century (see Chapter 3). Moreover, several of these languages were exported to other parts of the world as well, as a result of European colonization. This process might be called European nation-building overseas, in that the colonies were exploited for the benefit of European nations. In the era Europe went global, the continent created countries which were so extensive that they were called empires on which the sun never sets. This was true indeed, as at least one part of the territory was always in daylight. Originally used for the Spanish Empire in the sixteenth and seventeenth centuries, in the nineteenth and early twentieth centuries the phrase was used for the British Empire, which reached a size larger than that of any other empire in history. After both world wars, which left the old continent devastated, the United States took over the leading role in the world, strengthening the position of English as the most widely spoken language in the world.

As we discussed earlier, the concept of language is rather fuzzy, and so are the names ascribed to languages. Moreover, the division between languages as well as the division between languages and dialects is based on political rather than linguistic criteria. Therefore, variants which are very similar may be called the same language, whereas other, equally similar varieties may be called different languages. In 2017, the US Library of Congress,[4] which lists all languages in the world, recognized Montenegrin as a separate language and assigned it a language code. The decision came nine years after Montenegro, one of the constituent republics of former Yugoslavia and now an independent state, applied for international codification of its language. At first, the application was rejected, as Montenegrin was considered a variant of Serbian. The decision to recognize Montenegrin as a separate language was fiercely criticized outside the republic. According to the Head of the Library of the Serbian Academy of Sciences and Arts,[5] the recognition of Montenegrin was all about politics, not linguistics or science. When I asked a young university student from Montenegro, she proudly identified herself as a speaker of Montenegrin, a language she considered to be different from Serbian. Another interviewee from neighbouring Serbia disagreed, as she did not consider Montenegrin to be a separate language at all. According to her, there is hardly any difference between Serbian and Montenegrin. From a purely linguistic point of view, one could argue that the *Abstand* between Serbian and Montenegrin is very small indeed, while their *Ausbau* is far more significant – that is, the differences between the varieties are maximized on purpose. For instance, there have been attempts to artificially distance Montenegrin from Serbian through modifications to orthography and the introduction of new graphemes in particular. Anyway, the example shows that ordinary language users as well as linguists may find it very difficult to agree about the names of the languages they speak and whether they speak the same language or not.

Unfortunately, there are more confusing terms. The term 'world language' is a fuzzy concept too. It suggests that a particular language is used all over the world, which is obviously not the case. As a matter of fact, there is not a single language in the world which could claim this status, not even English. English may be the most widely used language in the world when combining all people who speak it as a native and as a non-native language. Unfortunately, the word 'native speaker' is particularly problematic, as the difference between 'native' and 'non-native' speakers tends to be a matter of interpretation and bias, and often intersects with race and perceived development. Many speakers from India or Kenya, to name but two Commonwealth countries, regard themselves as native speakers of English, even though many of them would classify as L2 speakers (speakers of English as a second language). Therefore, it may be safer to refer to first, second, or third language, even though this may lead to problems too. By number of people who speak it as a first language (L1), then, English probably is the third largest language worldwide, after Chinese (Mandarin) and Spanish. If one takes into account second language (L2) speakers as well, English beats all other languages.

Even though only 4 per cent of the languages spoken in the world are actually spoken in Europe, the continent's languages feature prominently in the top ten of the world's most widely spoken languages: English, Spanish, French, Russian, and Portuguese. These languages are the languages of former colonial powers (in Europe as well as other continents) who exported their languages all over their empires. Three of these languages (English, Spanish, and Portuguese) even have more speakers in countries other than the countries in which they originated. The languages of two former world players are conspicuously absent from this list: German, even though it is the most widely spoken L1 in Europe, and Dutch, the language of a small country which had a huge empire in the past. The other five languages in the top ten are spoken in the Far East and in Asia: Chinese, Hindi, Arabic, Bengali, and Malay. Unlike the European languages, these languages remained more or less confined to their continent, where they have millions of speakers. Africa and the American continent are completely absent from the top ten, as they adopted (that is, they were forced to adopt) European languages. The first African language in the list is Swahili (also known as Kiswahili),[6] with almost 100 million speakers (16 million as an L1, 82 million as an L2). While English is dominant in North America, Central and South America are dominated by Spanish. This is what the top ten based on number of speakers looks like (both L1 and L2):

TABLE 5.2 Top ten world languages (*Ethnologue*, 2019)[7]

Language	L1 speakers	L1 ranking	L2 speakers	L2 ranking	Total L1 + L2
English	379.0 million	3	753.3 million	1	1,132 billion
Chinese	917.8	1	198.7	5	1,116 billion
Hindi	341.2	4	274.2	2	615.4 million
Spanish	460.1	2	74.2	10	534.3 million
French	77.2	14	202.6	4	279.8 million
Arabic (standard)	–	–	273.9	3	273.9 million
Bengali	228.3	5	36.7	13	265.0 million
Russian	153.7	7	104.4	7	258.1 million
Portuguese	220.7	6	13.4	15	234.1 million
Malay	43.3	28	155.3	6	198.6 million

The numbers in the list should be regarded as indicative rather than absolute for the simple reason that it is impossible to count all speakers of a language. Moreover, information on the number of speakers is often not reliable (depending on the source) and there is no uniform way of counting speakers. As observed earlier, the boundaries between languages are not absolute either. In addition, some languages may be called dialects, and some dialects languages. What the languages in the top ten have in common is that they represent imagined communities: they are strong markers of identity and unity, as they embody linguistic, cultural, religious, economic, and political entities.

Unfortunately, the top ten of languages is based on number of speakers only, and it does not take into account other factors which determine the ultimate power of a language. The Power Language Index,[8] which was devised by the Chinese-Canadian economist Kai L. Chan, addresses some of these other issues. According to Chan, the power of a language depends on five categories (or opportunities, as he calls them): geography, economy, communication, knowledge and media, and diplomacy. Each of these domains is linked to a number of indicators (20 in total) which measure the usefulness of a particular language. 'Geography' refers to the countries in which the language is spoken, its territory, and the number of inbound tourists. 'Economy' discusses the country's GDP, its exports, the foreign exchange market, and the foreign exchange assets. 'Communication' is based on the number of native speakers, L2 speakers, the size of the language family, and outbound tourism. 'Knowledge and media' deals with the availability of internet sites in a given language, feature films produced in a country, its universities in the top 500, and academic journals in the language. Last but not least, 'diplomacy' measures to what extent a language is used in international organizations (IMF, UN, World Bank). The index should be understood as a snapshot of the current power of languages. That is, it does not reflect past trends nor does it say anything about the future. This is what the current top ten looks like (the numbers indicate the ranking of a language in the various domains):

TABLE 5.3 Top ten Power Language Index[9]

Language	Geography	Economy	Communication	Knowledge and media	Diplomacy
English	1	1	1	1	1
Chinese	6	2	2	3	6
French	2	6	5	5	1
Spanish	3	5	3	7	3
Arabic	4	9	6	18	4
Russian	5	12	10	9	5
German	8	3	7	4	8
Japanese	27	4	22	6	7
Portuguese	7	19	13	12	9
Hindi	13	16	8	2	10

The Power Language Index shows that English ranks first in all categories. Unfortunately, the index has not been updated since 2016, when it was created (an update is scheduled for 2019). If it were replicated, Chan reckons that Arabic might have diminished in importance, along with Japanese. The reason for Arabic declining would be prolonged depressed oil prices, which has diminished the economic might of Arabic-speaking countries, whereas Japan is on a slow-motion decline because of its ageing and shrinking population. English and Chinese (Mandarin) would be on the rise. Whereas English keeps getting stronger as it benefits from globalization, China's economy keeps growing and its linkages to the global economy continue to get deeper. Korean (presently 16th) and German seem to have gained in prominence too. However, it is not clear whether these changes would actually change the rank ordering.[10] Chan adds that the 2016 index 'likely underestimated' the power of English, which has become the second language in most countries, as a result of which being bilingual is usually taken to mean fluency in one's home language and English.[11]

By and large, the ranking in the 2016 Power Language Index is quite similar to the top ten of world languages based on *Ethnologue*: English is by far the most powerful language, followed by Chinese (Mandarin). French comes in third, surpassing Spanish. Two other languages enter the top ten: German and Japanese, which is mainly due to their economic power. On the other hand, two languages do not make it to the list of powerful languages: Malay and Bengali. The Power Language Index is dominated by six languages which originated in Europe, while the remaining four languages are used in the vast area between the Middle East and the Far East (for non-European readers, these terms may reflect a Eurocentric worldview). Africa appears to be the most powerless continent, as its languages are almost completely absent from the index.

The top ten of languages

Based on the Power Language Index (PLI) and *Ethnologue*, this part discusses the most powerful languages in the world, as well as two languages which are not so powerful from a global perspective but which belong to the most widely spoken languages worldwide due to the sheer size of their population, and one language which is relatively powerful even though it has far less speakers than the languages in the top ten.

What the languages in the top ten have in common is that they represent the major civilizations in the world. As argued by Huntington,[12] civilizations are bound to clash as the primary source of conflicts worldwide will increasingly be along cultural and religious lines. In the post-Cold War world, Western civilization is not as dominant as it used to be, and other civilizations have become important actors in shaping world history. Huntington divides the world into nine major civilizations: Western civilization (United States and Canada, Western and Central Europe, Australia, Oceania), in which English is the dominant language; Latin America, in which Spanish is dominant (Latin America may also be considered a part of Western civilization, as they share a Western Christian – Catholic or Protestant – culture); the Orthodox world (former Soviet Union, former Yugoslavia, etc.), in which Russian is or used to be dominant; the Eastern world, which consists of four civilizations and major languages (Buddhist, Hindu, Chinese, Japonic); and the Islamic world (Middle East, parts of Asia, northern Africa, Eastern Europe), in which Arabic serves as the language of religion. Sub-Saharan Africa (in which Swahili is one of the main languages) can be considered a ninth civilization. The demarcation lines between these civilizations are not always entirely clear. Moreover, there are some 'cleft countries' which belong to separate civilizations (e.g. Ukraine, Tanzania, the Philippines), and some 'lone countries' which have their own civilization (e.g. Ethiopia, Haiti, Israel). Conflicts between civilizations typically occur at the fault lines between them. A good example is former Yugoslavia, a cleft country (cleft in all senses of the word) where the Western, Orthodox and Islamic civilizations clash. Last but not least, it should be noted that some languages are widely used in several civilizations (e.g. English, French, Spanish, Portuguese).

English

English ranks first in all five domains of the PLI. Consequently, it is the most powerful language in the world. Its power is due to the legacy of the British Empire, but in particular to the economic, cultural, and military strength of the United States. Even though English is the most widely spoken language worldwide, it has less L1 speakers than Chinese and Spanish. English is spoken as an L1 in the United States (261 million), the United Kingdom (56 million), Canada (19 million), Australia (18 million), South Africa (almost 5 million), Ireland (4 million), New Zealand (almost 4 million), and in more than 100 other countries and territories worldwide.[13] If one includes the number of L2 speakers, the total rises easily over 1 billion. One might be tempted to conclude that the whole world speaks English. In many parts of the world, however, English is hardly used at all, and is not the lingua franca (i.e. a common language) it is often believed to be. Yet it cannot be denied that in many parts of the world, English is being used as a lingua franca indeed. This is especially the case in the areas of the world taking part in the process which is called globalization. Yet many areas do not take part in this process, as a consequence of which globalization is not as 'global' as the term suggests. Globalization basically is a process driven by the ideology of neo-liberalism, which favours free-market capitalism. A free market needs a common language to increase its efficiency, and English, the language of the most powerful economy in the world, serves this purpose well. In other words, the use of English as the world's most dominant language is due to economics and politics, not linguistics. The term 'world language' is not only confined by geography, but also by history. The fact that English achieved its current status as a world language is a mere coincidence, and it is highly unlikely it will retain this status forever. As nations rise and fall, languages come and go too. Yet English is not the language of one particular nation,

54 Language is politics

but of globalization. Even if China or another nation is to take over the role of the United States, English is likely to remain the world's working language. This will also be the case in the European Union after Brexit (i.e. the exit of the United Kingdom). The United Kingdom may not need Europe (as many believe), but Europe needs English.

Chinese (Mandarin)

Mandarin Chinese ranks second in the PLI, but it is only half as potent as English. Even if all Chinese languages/dialects were combined, this would not change the ranking. The rise of Chinese is a relatively recent phenomenon, dating back to its emergence as a world player in the post-Mao era. As a first language, Chinese is the most widely spoken language in the world. Yet the number of Chinese speakers may be particularly misleading, as Chinese is a so-called *macrolanguage* consisting of dozens of different forms and dialects which are not mutually intelligible. Many of these varieties could be regarded as different languages, but for political and cultural reasons, including the use of a common script, they are regarded as one language. Varieties of Chinese are spoken all over Asia and in the Chinese diaspora worldwide. Mandarin Chinese is the most common variety, which is spoken by some 70 per cent of its speakers. Due to the nature of its written form (the so-called characters), Chinese is accessible to a much larger audience than its spoken forms. Chinese, Japanese, and Koreans can – to a certain extent – communicate due to the common linguistic root of written Chinese. In the 1950s, the Chinese communist regime introduced simplified characters to improve literacy rates, while the anti-communist refugees in Taiwan continued the use of traditional characters. Traditional characters are also used in Hong Kong and Macau. Since their handover to mainland China, the new government has promoted the use of Mandarin Chinese. The question whether the emergence of China as a global power will improve the position of its language is not so easy to answer. First of all, Chinese is difficult to learn for many foreigners because of its complex writing system. There are over 50,000 characters in Chinese, of which an educated Chinese person will know about 8,000. In order to be able to read a newspaper, one will need between 2,000 and 3,000 characters. As far as the spoken language is concerned, the problem is that Chinese is a tonal language. A tonal language has different 'tones' (like pitches in music) which change the meaning of a word. 'Ma', for instance, can mean mother (mā, 妈), but also, depending on the tone, 'hemp' (má, 麻), 'horse' (mǎ, 马), 'scold' (mà, 骂),[14] and it can indicate a question (吗) when put at the end of a sentence (e.g. nǐ hǎo ma? 你好吗 In English: How are you? – literally 'You good?'). Whereas Mandarin has four tones (as well as an additional 'neutral' tone in questions), Cantonese has nine. For speakers of languages without tones (such as Western languages), the system is very difficult to grasp. Even though Chinese face similar problems when learning English, in general it is easier to learn English than Chinese. It may be safe to bet that the Chinese will know English before most other people have started learning Chinese.

French

French ranks third in the PLI thanks to its prestige in international diplomacy (even though English clearly is the de facto working language). Like English, French has a high number of L2 speakers, particularly in Africa. The origin of French is in the variety of Romance spoken in Gaul, led by the dialect of Île-de-France in the Paris area. French is an official language in 29 countries, including France (60 million L1 speakers), Canada (in Quebec, 7 million L1), Belgium (in Wallonia and Brussels, 4 million L1), and the western part of Switzerland (almost 2 million L1).[15] As a result of French and Belgian colonialism, French was introduced in the Americas, Africa, and Asia. After France, the Democratic Republic of Congo is home to the second largest French-speaking population in the world (9 million). As colonizers, the French were convinced of their *mission civilisatrice*, the belief in the superiority of the French culture and language, which as a result had to be introduced in all of their territories. This policy was very different from the British language policy, which generally promoted the use of local languages rather than the colonial language.[16] The French saw evidence of their excellence in the French language itself, and they set up the first academy in the world dedicated to the care of a language, the *Académie française*. Throughout the seventeenth and eighteenth centuries, the prestige of French was enormous, and it served as the language of the elite in countries as diverse as Sweden, Poland, and Russia. The dominance of French as the language of high culture and diplomacy lasted until the 1919 peace conference held after the First World War, when the Americans and British insisted on using English, as a result of which the peace treaty was published in both French and English.[17] One hundred years later, the leading role of French has almost completely been taken over by English.

Spanish

The global reach of Spanish remains limited as it is spoken only in Europe and Latin America, where it is the most widely spoken language. As the latter continent grows, Spanish may eclipse French in the PLI. European Spanish came about as an alliance of Galician, Castilian, and Catalan, but it is mostly identified as Castilian, the language of the most powerful region. Currently, Spanish has far more speakers in Latin America than in Europe where the language originated. The Spanish conquistadores exported their language and religion to America, which was 'discovered' by Columbus in 1492. As pointed out by the Uruguayan writer Eduardo Galeano,[18] the Spaniards accomplished their mission by means of a coalition between the *sword* (the king's army) and the *cross* (the Catholic Church), representing the Spanish state. In the course of the ruthless Spanish colonization, indigenous languages and their speakers were driven back or wiped out. Today, Mexico is the country with most Spanish speakers (almost 120 million). In Spain, the number of L1 speakers is estimated at 42 million. Other important Hispanophone countries include Colombia (47 million), Argentina (42 million), and Venezuela (30 million).[19] The United States should be mentioned here too (probably 43 million), where its use is contested by the English Only movement, a group of neocons which feels threatened by the surge of Spanish (see Chapter 7). Even though the varieties of Spanish are generally mutually intelligible, there are many lexical and grammatical differences between them, and the pronunciation is different too.

Arabic (Modern Standard Arabic)

The strong position of Arabic in the PLI is mainly due to the number of countries in which Arabic is spoken as well as its use as an official language in international organizations. On the other hand, its position as a language of knowledge and media remains rather weak. Arabic is spoken primarily in the Middle East and North Africa (MENA). Like Chinese, Arabic is a macrolanguage whose standard form serves as the lingua franca of the Arab world. Arabic consists of many different spoken varieties, which are not always mutually intelligible. For political reasons, however, Arabs will commonly assert that they speak a single language.[20] Arabic can be regarded as a continuum in which speakers constantly switch between different varieties and genres. While the standard variety is confined to formal contexts, in daily life people speak their local dialects. For instance, an Arab nation such as Egypt has its own varieties of Arabic. Egypt's second president, Gamal Abdel Nasser, the iconic leader who led the overthrow of the monarchy in 1952 and who called for pan-Arabic unity, typically switched between Standard Arabic and the Egyptian variety of Arabic in his speeches. Apart from its political function, Arabic plays an important role as the language of Islam. It has even been argued that without Arabic, Islam is unimaginable.[21] Like the Chinese writing system, the Arabic script serves as a marker of identity, and it can be read by speakers who cannot always communicate when speaking. Thus, the Arabic script acts as a lingua franca in itself. In Islamic countries in which Arabic is not present in daily life or not spoken at all, it is nevertheless present in a religious context. This is the case in Turkey and in many other Islamic countries. Among the elites in the Arab world, however, English is often seen as the language of prestige, and even given preference over Arabic.

Russian

Russian is widely spoken in many countries of the former Soviet Union and its satellite states, in many of which related Slavic languages are spoken. In spite of its rather poor economic ranking in the PLI, Russia remains a powerful nation. Most speakers of Russian live in the Russian Federation (119 million L1), with smaller populations in Ukraine (14 million), Belarus (6.6 million), Uzbekistan (4 million), and Kazakhstan (3.7 million).[22] From the sixteenth century onwards, Russian language policy entailed the *Russification* of their territories in Asia and Europe. When the soviets took over from the tsars in 1917, the new rulers decided there would be no official language, as all peoples of the Union were to be equal.[23] In practice, however, Russian remained the only possible lingua franca for the vast empire. After the collapse of the Soviet Union in 1992, the prospects for Russian looked rather bleak. In several of its former republics, English has taken over the role of an L2. This is, for instance, what happened in the Baltic states. The same could be observed in their former allies in Eastern Europe, which have also switched to English. Also, in Cuba, which was largely dependent on Russian aid because of the US embargo, English is now more widely taught than Russian. It should be noted that Russian never achieved the prestige of languages such as French, German, and English, not even in Russia.[24] In contrast to the other European languages in the top ten, Russian uses the Cyrillic alphabet, the use of which was expanded to other languages (e.g. Kazakh and Mongolian) in soviet times. Today, one may observe a push to adopt the Latin script, which is considered less politically sensitive (and which looks more Western).

German

In spite of its small geographic coverage worldwide, German places seventh on the PLI. This position is mainly due to the strength of the economies of the German-speaking countries. In spite of the fact that Germany played a major role in world history, the language of the European hegemon never attained the world status of English or French. Yet the German language is the most widely spoken L1 in Europe, with more speakers (roughly 76 million) than English or French.[25] In addition, German is spoken by 56 million speakers as an L2, which is considerably less than English or French. The language is spoken as an L1 in Germany, Austria, the main part of Switzerland (alongside Swiss German), Luxembourg (alongside Luxemburgish), and Liechtenstein. Furthermore, German is a recognized language in the east of Belgium, South Tyrol in Italy, and in the south of Denmark. The German language area has many dialectical variations, and some of the dialects are not mutually intelligible. Apart from its use in Western Europe, German served as a lingua franca in Eastern Europe before being replaced by Russian (after the Second World War) and English (after the implosion of the Soviet Union). Whereas English and French are spoken all over the world, German essentially remained a European language. This may be due to Germany's geographical position in the centre of Europe as well as the fact that Germany was unified as late as 1871. When Germany appeared on the world stage as a colonizer, most of the cake had been divided already. The German colonies included Togoland (now part of Ghana and Togo), Cameroon, German East Africa (now Rwanda, Burundi, and Tanzania), and German South West Africa (now Namibia). After its defeat in the First World War in 1918, Germany lost all its overseas territories and the German language was replaced by the languages of the new colonizers. In contrast to the French, German speakers seldom forced foreigners to adopt their language.[26]

Japanese

Japanese is the most isolated language in the PLI's top ten (hence its 27th place in the category of geography). Also, in terms of communication, Japan ranks quite low

(22nd). From an economic point of view, Japan is still relatively powerful (4th), but in general its influence is likely to wane over time. This is due to declining birth rates and lack of immigration as well as economic stagnation. Perhaps most important of all, the Japanese language is spoken in Japan only, a country which for a very long time pursued an isolationist foreign policy. Between 1600 and 1886, nearly all foreigners were barred from entering the country while the Japanese could not leave their country. For most foreign learners, Japanese is a complex language, which has limited its uptake as an L2. Japanese uses three writing systems (*katakana*, *hiragana*, and *kanji*) as well as the Latin alphabet for transliterations (called *rōmaji*). Even though Chinese people can read kanji (basically Chinese characters used in Japanese), they may not always understand them, as the characters do not necessarily have the same meaning. While hiragana is used primarily for grammatical purposes such as verb inflections, katakana is used for words imported from foreign languages (e.g. メール, 'mēru' borrowed from the English word 'email'). The sentence 学生は食べます ('gakusei wa tabemasu'), which translates in English as 'the student(s) eat', combines kanji (学生, 'the student', and 食, 'eat') and hiragana (は, the particle 'wa' to define the topic, and べます, the verb inflection).

Portuguese

Like English and Spanish, Portuguese is most prominent outside its historic homeland. Portuguese is related to Galician, a language spoken in the north-western part of Spain bordering Portugal. Portugal has far less speakers of Portuguese (11 million) than its former colony Brazil (over 200 million). Portuguese is also the official language of Cape Verde, Guinea-Bissau, Mozambique, Angola, and São Tomé and Príncipe. Besides, it has co-official status in East Timor, Equatorial Guinea, and Macau. Portuguese creole speakers are to be found in various places in the Indian subcontinent (e.g. in Goa and Flores) and in the Caribbean (the Lesser Antilles). The fact that Brazil became a Portuguese rather than a Spanish colony could be called a coincidence. A dispute between both colonial powers was settled by the 1494 Treaty of Tordesillas, which granted Portugal all lands east of a meridian line 370 leagues west of the Cape Verde islands.[27] As the Tordesillas line ran across Brazil, the country was granted to Portugal. Like their Spanish neighbours, the Portuguese were driven to convert their territories to the Catholic religion. Whereas the Portuguese managed to transplant their language effectively in their largest colony, Brazil, it was less successful in their other colonies, where it was widely pidginised.[28]

Hindi

Sometimes Hindi and Urdu are listed as one language. Whereas the PLI concedes that Hindi and Urdu are essentially the same language, it lists them as two different languages (ranking 10th and 30th, respectively). The distinction between Hindi and Urdu symbolizes the rift between India and Pakistan and their independence from

British governance in 1947. Whereas Hindi was promoted as the official language of India, alongside with English, Urdu serves as the national language of Pakistan. They use different scripts, and since the partition of India and Pakistan they have developed their own unique features. The controversy regarding the status of Hindi and Urdu as a single language or as two varieties of a single language remains an ongoing controversy.[29] Mahatma Gandhi, the leader of the independence movement, deplored the Hindu–Muslim divide, and he proposed remerging the standards under the traditional generic term Hindustani. Apart from Hindi/Urdu, hundreds of other languages are spoken in the Indian subcontinent, many with millions of L1 speakers, such as Bengali (228 million), Marathi (83 million), Telugu (82 million), Tamil (75 million), Gujarati (56 million), and Punjabi (32 million).[30] Contrary to what one might expect, only 30 per cent of the population in India speaks English. The former colonial language mainly serves as the language of the elite. They send their children to English private schools, whereas the vast majority send theirs to government schools where instruction is in the local language. Even though many states in India have attempted to introduce English as their medium of instruction, there is a shortage of teachers who can actually teach in English. One might argue that a new, linguistic caste system has emerged.[31] Also, in higher education, the use of English remains problematic, and many students from the former British Empire face serious problems when studying in an English-speaking context abroad, even though they regard themselves as 'native' speakers of English.

The number of speakers a language has does not necessarily correlate with its global power. Although Malay and Bengali feature in the list of the most widely spoken languages in the world, they are conspicuously absent in the top ten of the most powerful languages.

Malay

Malay is a polycentric language with several standards which are not mutually intelligible. It uses the Latin script (Rumi), although a modified Arabic script (Jawi) also exists. Rumi is official in Indonesia, Malaysia, and Singapore. Malay ranks 14th in the PLI, its only real asset being the number of speakers it has in South East Asia. Moreover, Malay is known under different names: in Indonesia, it is called *Bahasa Indonesia* (Indonesian language); in Malaysia, *Bahasa Malaysia* (Malaysian language); and in Singapore and Brunei, *Bahasa Melayu* (Malay language). It may be a surprise that the lingua franca of modern Indonesia is a form of Malay rather than Dutch, the language of the former colonizer. There is some irony in the fact that Malay was actually promoted by the Dutch, who did not impose their own language, as most other colonizers did. This has been attributed to what Nicholas Ostler[32] referred to as the 'strange unwillingness of the Dutch to share their language with their colonial subjects', which will be discussed later. Malay actually served as a lingua franca, which was also adopted by the Dutch colonizers.

Bengali

Bengali (also known as Bangla) is only 39th on the PLI, which is mainly due to its confined geography and its weak economic position. Bengali is the official and most widely spoken language of Bangladesh as well as an important marker of the nation's identity. It is also the second most widely spoken language in India. Bengali was made the national language of Bangladesh in 1971, replacing English in most domains, including education. Many original English-medium universities, schools, and colleges converted to Bengali instruction in order to spread mass education. Due to the widespread use of Bengali, the former colonial language lost its official status and dominance. However, English still plays a significant role as a working language and as a language of wider communication, especially in an elite context. Like in India, the use of English in higher education remains problematic, and many students from Bangladesh face serious problems when studying in an English-speaking context abroad.

In contrast to Malay and Bengali, a language can have relatively few speakers worldwide and yet be quite powerful. A good example is Dutch, a language with only 23 million speakers worldwide (mainly in the Netherlands and Belgium), which ranks 13th on the PLI, right after Cantonese (80 million speakers) and Italian (67 million speakers).

Dutch

In spite of its being a small European state, the Netherlands played a major role as a colonizer all over the world. Today, Dutch is mainly spoken in the Low Countries (the Netherlands and Belgium), as well as in Surinam (Dutch Guiana) and the former Dutch Antilles. In contrast to the Spanish colonization, which was organized by 'the sword and the cross', or the French *mission civilisatrice*, Dutch colonization was pragmatic and mainly informed by commercial interests. The Dutch basic concern was in making profit and a better life, not in exporting their language or culture. Dutch pragmatism called for the use of a foreign contact language which was available already (such as Malay in the Dutch Indies) rather than their own language.[33] It should be noted that the Dutch East India Company (VOC) was a corporation and not an institution set up for the benefit of the king and the Church, as was the case in Spain. When Dutch was introduced after all (as in the former Dutch Antilles), this was because there was no other language available as a lingua franca. In South Africa, Dutch even developed into a completely new standard language, which is unique in colonial history.[34] Originally, Afrikaans was the language of Dutch farmers (*boer* in Dutch, hence Boer War in English) which later came to be associated with apartheid. Today, the Dutch are the frontrunners of introducing English in their country, for instance in higher education, again at the expense of their own language. It has been argued that the Dutch are not interested in their language. According to Dutch sociologist Abram de Swaan, the Dutch attitude is due to their character, which he describes as indifferent towards the language issue and 'bordering on cultural self-effacement and even self-contempt'.[35] Recently, De Swaan argued that the situation in the Netherlands has even deteriorated and that the voluntary and institutional switch to English is motivated by commercial arguments only.[36]

Apart from the languages discussed here, there are many other languages with millions of speakers. One of these languages is Turkish, 18th in the PLI with some 75 million speakers. It is the most widely spoken of the Turkic languages, a language family covering a vast land mass ranging from Eurasia all the way to East Asia. It has been argued that one could travel all the way from Europe to Asia while speaking some kind of Turkish with small modifications as one goes along. Even though this may be an exaggeration, it illustrates the point that languages in fact do not exist, but that they are modifications along a continuum of dialects. Moreover, Turkish is spoken in many other parts of the world as well. Due to migration, large numbers of Turkish speakers are scattered over the West. It has been claimed that Berlin would be the largest Turkish city outside of Turkey, but this is most probably a myth.

Language and power

Another way to understand the power relations between languages is provided by the Global Language System, which was developed by Abram de Swaan in 2001.[37] De Swaan divides the world's languages into a hierarchy of four levels: peripheral, central, supercentral, and hypercentral languages. According to De Swaan, the 'peripheral' languages of the early agrarian societies were grouped together by new rulers who imposed their own language, as a result of which the first 'central' languages emerged. A good example is Latin, which emerged from Rome and which developed into a central language in Europe. Similarly, Chinese, Sanskrit, and Arabic became central languages in other parts of the world. Some of these languages developed into 'supercentral' languages, as they were spread by land and sea as a result of military and other conquests. Historically, the core nations in this respect were to be found in the north-west of Europe, including England and France. These pre-capitalist nations colonized many other nations between the fifteenth and nineteenth centuries, and they also 'exported' their languages to every corner of the world. Due to the growing dominance of the United States after the Second World War, English emerged as the 'hypercentral' language and the tool of globalization.

In today's world, peripheral languages are mainly local languages with an oral tradition and a limited number of speakers (some languages may have a handful to some hundred speakers or more), which may be found in developing countries. Some of these languages are often not considered proper languages as they are not well described or because they lack prestige, and they may be known under different names. For example, Aruhuaco[39] (also known as Ika and more than ten other names) is one of the many indigenous languages spoken in Colombia. Its population is around 8,000 speakers, most of whom are monolingual. They live in a mountainous area, remote from cities and a Spanish-speaking environment.

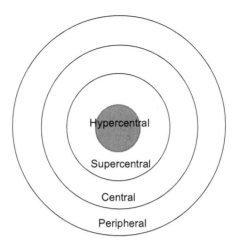

FIGURE 5.1 The Global Language System[38]

Aruhuaco boasts a strong traditional culture and is nowadays taught in primary schools, thus ensuring its survival. In contrast to Aruhuaco, many other peripheral languages all over the world are endangered, and many have ceased to exist. The fact that a language has only a limited number of speakers who often live in remote areas does not necessarily imply that these communities are cut off from the world. While most speakers of Aruhuaco live high in the mountains, far away from the nearest villages, and they live in traditional villages where they wear their typical white dresses and hats, some of them have smartphones and access to the internet, where they conduct web searches in Spanish and maybe in English. Thus, traditional societies may have access to the world and the world's dominant languages. A peripheral language can be spoken in several countries, and it can have millions of speakers. A good example of the latter is Quechua, a macrolanguage spoken mainly in Peru, but also by significant populations in Ecuador, Bolivia, Chile, Colombia, and Argentina. Quechua has more than 7 million speakers.[40]

Central languages are well described, they serve as the language of larger communities such as nations or nation-states, and some of them have millions of speakers. Many of these languages are used as official languages of a country or a larger community, such as the European Union. Also, many languages spoken in Asia and Africa can be considered central languages, even if they may not be well known internationally. Supercentral languages have the same characteristics as central languages, but they have more speakers (tens of millions) and they have more power in an international context. Often they are not just official languages, but working languages as well. This holds for French or German in the European Union, or Russian in the Russian Federation. The other languages mentioned in the top ten may be considered supercentral languages as well, in that they serve as lingua francas, often of vast multilingual states. As the only hypercentral language in the world, English overshadows all other languages. It is used by hundreds of

FIGURE 5.2 Aruhuaco
Source: Anne Walraet

millions of people with various levels of proficiency in various domains of society. The main advantage of English is its communicative value, which is greater than any other language in the world.

The present Global Language System is a relatively recent phenomenon. Moreover, it is a European phenomenon, as the very concept of standard languages, on which the Global Language System is based, was coined in Europe. As observed earlier, languages were used to shape nations, and languages were shaped too, to preserve the myth that they really exist. Therefore, languages were standardized, codified, and made different from other languages. Moreover, the standard languages used in Europe are all central languages representing powerful and competing nation-states.

In seventeenth-century Europe, French emerged as the continent's supercentral language. As pointed out already, French gained ground as the language of the highest ranks of society, such as the court and the nobility. The French language made it as far as the Russian court, where it became associated with ideas of progress and Europeanness. French also served as the language of diplomacy, scientific knowledge, and good taste in general. Substantial parts of Tolstoy's *War and Peace* were not written in Russian, but in French. Even Leibniz, the German scientist, wrote all his major works in French.[41] The prestige of French as the lingua franca of the elite spread over the continent well into the nineteenth and twentieth centuries, when other languages, in particular German and English, challenged its position.

German unification in 1871 shifted the power relations in Europe. After the nationalistic war against France, Germany developed into a self-conscious nation-state, based on the concepts of people, territory, and language. Standard German developed as the nation's supercentral language, which also gained considerable prestige in other countries (e.g. in the Scandinavian countries and the Netherlands, where German played a significant role as a language of science and education). The German language achieved world prominence, equalling French. The ideas of the Enlightenment were first expressed in German, the language of Goethe, Schiller, Beethoven, and Mozart. By 1890, Germany was arguably the strongest power in Europe, foreshadowing both the First and Second World Wars, when the clash between Europe's great nations almost destroyed the continent.

The end of the Second World War marked the end of the dominant European languages as well, in particular German and French. German military defeat had a devastating effect on the German language and culture and its perception abroad. In spite of the huge influence of its writers and thinkers in the past, German lost its prestige in the world. Due to anti-German sentiment after the war, German books were burned in huge public bonfires, mirroring former Nazi practices.[42] The war led to the end of German as an international and scientific language. Scholars and refugees from Germany and Austria emigrated to the United States, where they adopted English as their new language. A good example may be German-born Albert Einstein, who became an American citizen in 1940. Throughout his entire life, Einstein spoke English with a very strong German accent.[43] In the German-speaking countries, where English became more prominent after the war, the dominance of English was accepted more easily than in the French-speaking countries.

Even though the French had won the war, they lost their language too. Compared to the sudden downfall of German, the decline of French was a slow but undeniable process. French could no longer claim its pre-war status and gradually had to give way to English, the language of the United States, which emerged as the world's dominant power. The French found it particularly difficult to accept the hypercentrality of English and the loss of international prestige of their language. Therefore, the use of English words was officially discouraged or even forbidden, and French equivalents were suggested. The 1994 Toubon Law – which takes its name from Jacques Toubon, the then minister of culture – was passed to mandate the use of French in official government publications, advertisements, workplaces, schools, contracts, and so on. The law was nicknamed 'All good' in English (a literal translation of *Tout bon*) as its obvious aim was to curb the use of English in France. Much to the French chagrin, their anti-English language policy was never particularly successful.

To sum up, it was only after the Second World War that English emerged as the world's most dominant language. Moreover, the rise of English was not due to British hegemony, as the power of the former empire had reduced significantly, but it was entirely due to the role of the United States in the world. The power relations between both English-speaking countries had shifted dramatically: the United States has become the leading power in the world, while the former British Empire faces difficulties in coming to terms with its reduced status in the world.

Notes

1. Eberhard et al. (2019).
2. See: www.sil.org (accessed 5 March 2019).
3. Eberhard et al. (2019).
4. See: www.loc.gov/standards/iso639-2/php/English_list.php (accessed 18 February 2019).
5. See: www.b92.net/eng/news/region.php?yyyy=2017&mm=12&dd=14&nav_id=103042 (accessed 30 March 2018).
6. Kiswahili is the language of the Swahili people (the prefix ki- refers to language), but in English the language is often referred to as Swahili. Originally written in Arabic, the European colonizers changed the script to de-Arabize the language and to extricate the Islamic elements. For the story of Swahili, see Mugane (2015: 203).
7. Eberhard et al. (2019).
8. See: www.kailchan.ca/wp-content/uploads/2016/12/Kai-Chan_Power-Language-Index-full-report_2016_v2.pdf (accessed 8 February 2019).
9. See: www.kailchan.ca/wp-content/uploads/2016/12/Kai-Chan_Power-Language-Index-full-report_2016_v2.pdf (accessed 8 February 2019).
10. Kai L. Chan, personal communication, 8 March 2019.
11. See www.weforum.org/agenda/2018/11/is-english-too-powerful/ (accessed 25 January 2019).
12. Huntington (1996).
13. Numbers based on Eberhard et al. (2019).
14. The different tones in 'ma' can be heard here: www.thoughtco.com/four-tones-of-mandarin-2279480 (accessed 25 January 2019).
15. Eberhard et al. (2019).
16. Joseph (2006: 50).
17. Ostler (2006: 403–418).
18. Galeano (1971/1997).
19. Eberhard et al. (2019).
20. Habash (2010).
21. Ostler (2006: 537).
22. Eberhard et al. (2019).
23. Ostler (2006: 441).
24. Ostler (2006: 437).
25. Eberhard et al. (2019).
26. See: www.kailchan.ca/wp-content/uploads/2016/12/Kai-Chan_Power-Language-Index-full-report_2016_v2.pdf (accessed 8 February 2019).
27. Ostler (2006: 337, 385).
28. Ostler (2006: 391, 398).
29. Khan (2006).
30. Eberhard et al. (2019).
31. See: www.forbes.com/sites/realspin/2014/11/06/the-problem-with-the-english-language-in-india/#5aacff63403e (accessed 3 April 2018).
32. Ostler (2006: 402, footnote).
33. Groeneboer (1988).
34. De Swaan (2001).
35. De Swaan, 2001: 87).
36. De Swaan, personal communication, 28 May 2019.
37. De Swaan (2001).
38. De Swaan (2001).

39 See: www.language-archives.org/language/arh (accessed 5 March 2019).
40 Eberhard et al. (2019).
41 Ostler (2006: 410).
42 Wulf (2015: 336).
43 Einstein's comments on the language of science (and his strong German accent) can be heard at www.youtube.com/watch?v=gTlpJ9ue04w (accessed 2 February 2019).

6
THE POWER OF ENGLISH

English as a world language

There may be some irony in the fact that English, originally the language of the southern part of a relatively small island just off the European mainland, has developed into the most widely used language in the world. English may also be the most 'Frenchified' language in the world, in that a substantial portion of its vocabulary derives from Norman French, the language of William the Conqueror and the elite who ruled Britain for centuries. No one could have imagined that English, then the language of the common people, would become such a powerful language worldwide. Even though the historical context is entirely different, there is nevertheless a striking difference between the way French was imposed in Britain and the stubborn resistance to English in France.

The British colonial empire took shape relatively late compared to some other colonial powers. When the British arrived in the Americas, the south of the continent was already occupied by their Spanish and Portuguese rivals. The British had to be satisfied with the north, which was far less attractive in terms of natural resources. Whereas the Spaniards ruled their colonies with an iron fist and shipped off their natural reserves to Spain, the British colonizers developed 'inclusive' instead of 'extractive' institutions, eventually leading to prosperity in the north.[1] In other words, the colonizers of North America settled and invested in their new home country, whereas South America was depleted and its wealth invested in the Old World. The Spaniards also imposed their language and religion in the colonies, wielding the power of the state and the Church.[2] The British attitude was far more pragmatic and driven by commercial instinct, an attitude which they had in common with their Dutch rival colonizers. The fact that English eventually became the language of the United States can almost be called a coincidence. Legend has it that English defeated German by a single vote to become the country's official language.³ In fact, however, the United States has never had an official language, reflecting its overall liberal attitude towards language. It should be noted, however, that the attitude towards languages other than English is not always (and has not always been) liberal, as exemplified by the current tensions around the use of Spanish in the United States.

It has been argued that English is today's new Latin. Yet this comparison does not hold. Latin was mainly used as a means of written communication among a small intellectual elite in Europe, whereas English is used all over the world in all layers of society and in a huge variety of spoken and written forms. It may be relevant to compare English and Latin in more detail, however. Latin remained Europe's intellectual language until the end of the eighteenth century, when it lost its dominant position to the so-called vernaculars, the 'national' languages of the emerging nation-states. Most people continued to use their local dialects, which were all they needed in an age in which most people were illiterate anyway. The intellectual elite would have used at least two languages: apart from their local languages, which were initially used for everyday purposes only, Latin was used for writing and academic purposes, often in an international (i.e. European) context. The Collegium Trilingue, which might be called the first university language centre in Europe, was founded by Erasmus in Leuven (in today's Belgium) in 1519, reflecting an ambitious humanistic programme. According to Erasmus, trilingualism meant being fluent in Latin, Greek, and Hebrew, which he regarded as a prerequisite for academic success. One scholar who attained such success was Thomas More, the author of *Utopia*, a political satire which is still read widely today. The book was first published in Latin in 1516 and it was not until 1551 that it was translated into English. Galileo Galilei was among the best-known scientists who used their vernacular instead of Latin. These scientists invented many new words which were introduced as equivalents to the Latin terms (especially for mathematical and military concepts). The seventeenth-century natural philosopher Robert Boyle argued that even the most obscure problems, whether in astronomy or in chemistry, could be discussed in the national language instead of Latin. From then onwards, other languages began to gain prestige as languages of science, and books which had previously only been available in Latin were now being published in English, French, Italian, and so on. The last major work in England to be published in Latin was Newton's *Principia* (1687). Modern languages were taught from the sixteenth century onwards, though Latin remained important in education.

The current position of English may be challenged by other languages. Some argue that Chinese is the language of the future, as China is on the verge of surpassing the United States as the world's leading superpower. While this may be true, it seems unlikely that Chinese will replace English as a hypercentral language. The reason is that English is firmly rooted in everyday life all over the world: in commerce, politics, education, and culture. Moreover, as observed earlier, English is relatively easy to learn, which is not the case for Chinese. Due to linguistic inertia – the fact that relationships between languages change more slowly than the world around us – the supremacy of English looks likely to last for some time.

The current use of English by so many people all over the world is having a major impact on the language itself. Like Latin, English could develop into a number of related but distinct languages. In fact, this has already happened: some of the varieties of English used in some parts of the world are very difficult for speakers of other varieties to understand, even if they are considered standard English by their speakers. A useful way to classify the different varieties of English is the concentric circles model, which was developed by the Indian linguist Braj Kachru[4] in the 1980s. Kachru distinguishes three 'circles' of English: the norm-providing inner circle, which refers to the traditional bases of English (mainly the United Kingdom and the United States), the norm-developing outer circle, which includes regions where English plays an important role as a second language, often in a multilingual setting (e.g. India and other former colonies), and the norm-dependent expanding circle, where English is taught as a foreign language and acknowledged as an important language for international relations (e.g. China).

Although the concentric circles model has had a tremendous impact on teaching and research practices, it does have shortcomings. First of all, the model is an oversimplification of reality, and there are grey areas between the circles. South Africa, for example, can be regarded as either an inner circle or outer circle country, depending on the different linguistic background of speakers in the country. Bangladesh can be placed in either the outer circle or the expanding circle, as English is the language of its higher education system, but Bengali is the official language which played an important role in the construction of the national identity. In spite of its claim that all three circles are equally important, the model is commonly perceived to locate the inner circle and the native speakers at the centre of the model, a position which is disputed nowadays. As mentioned earlier,

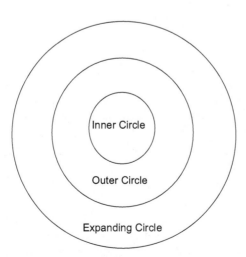

FIGURE 6.1 The concentric circles of English[5]

the term 'native speaker' entails a cultural bias, as it implicitly singles out Western and especially white speakers of English, even though English is used as a native language by speakers of all races on all continents.

The outer circle comprises regions where English serves as an official language and where it is present in daily life and spoken as a second language. Yet a language may be 'official' to varying degrees (e.g. it might be official in a limited number of domains or in combination with one or more other languages). Moreover, English is not present in everyone's daily lives (as many do not have access to English at all), whereas for other people in the outer circle, English serves as the first language. On the other hand, English is increasingly being used as a common language in the expanding circle, for instance in higher education. In several of these countries, English can hardly be called a foreign language anymore (e.g. in the Netherlands and Scandinavia), and new varieties of English are emerging, as a result of which these 'norm-dependent countries' may actually become 'norm-developing countries'. Due to globalization, the inner circle has become as linguistically complex as the other two circles, and increasing numbers of people do not speak English as a first language. In 2005, Kachru provided a more dynamic version of his model which allowed for overlap between the circles.[6] But still, the very concept of concentric circles does not account for today's complex multilingual and interlingual practices, commonly referred to as linguistic superdiversity.[7]

It should be noted that English is mainly used as a lingua franca among speakers for whom it is a second or third or whatever language. There may be some irony in the fact that speakers of related languages such as German and Dutch tend to communicate with each other in English, even though communication in their own languages could be possible, as the vocabulary and grammar of these languages are much closer to one another than to English. A similar tendency to use English rather than 'Scandinavian' can be observed in the Nordic countries. Speakers of English as a first language, meanwhile, are a minority internationally, but a powerful one, as they decide the rules of the language which are then codified in dictionaries, grammars, and style guides. They also control the English language teaching and testing industry, which has developed into a lucrative business.

The internationalization of English has led to a new controversy regarding the 'ownership' of English[8] in today's world: Which and whose language norms are to be adopted? This is a sensitive issue, as norms are ideologically loaded and culturally biased. As English becomes more international, it could also become more democratic, leading to the end of the current democratic deficit. The question, however, is: Who decides the new norms? As far as pronunciation is concerned, non-native English accents are commonly evaluated according to their proximity to inner circle accents, especially British and American accents. As a result, Scandinavian and Dutch accents, which sound relatively 'native-like' (i.e. British- or American-like), tend to be received more positively than other accents. Accents which are perceived as being more different from native English (e.g. Chinese English) are generally received negatively.[9] Similarly, there may be more tolerance towards non-native varieties of English whose grammatical and other features resemble inner circle English. For instance, it has been argued that Dutch English should be accepted as a variety of English in its own right, with its own phonological and grammatical features.[10] Thus, varieties of English which are more remote from inner circle English (including outer circle varieties such as Indian English) may be perceived as more 'deficient' than some expanding circle varieties of English (such as Dutch English). This may also be due to cultural factors. Thus, cultural and linguistic inner circle proximity may be a clear advantage, which may be obvious in an academic context in which Anglo-Saxon paradigms are clearly dominant.

The rise of English

There is no doubt that English is the most dominant language in the world. That is, it is the most dominant language *today*. There was a time when English was mainly a local language, and in the future other languages may become more dominant than English. Even today, English is not the most dominant language *everywhere* in the world. In the outer circle, the prominence of English dates back to the time when Britannia ruled the waves, but its emergence in the expanding circle can be attributed to Uncle Sam's role in the world after the First and Second World Wars. Not all parts of the world were affected equally by the rise of English, and neither were all domains of communication. International business and politics were quick to adopt English as a lingua franca, for example, but it was only much later that higher education followed suit. These issues will be discussed in the next sections. But first, let's consider the role of English on the internet, in books, in films, and in *Snow White*.

In internet surveys listing the most influential books in history, we see a strong bias towards books written in English by twentieth-century male writers. One such survey lists 14 books written in English, three in German, one in French, one in Italian, and one in ancient Greek. Of these 14, 11 books were written after 1900 and only one was written by a woman.[11] Of course, the internet is mainly in English. When it started, it was even English only, reflecting the origins of the internet: the US federal government, whose aim was to build robust computer communication. Even though other languages have become prominent on the internet too, it has been predicted that English will retain its dominant position.[12] Similarly, most books and films are known by their English titles. Thus, Sigmund Freud's *Traumdeutung* has become *The Interpretation of Dreams* and Jean-Paul Sartre's *L'Être et le Néant* has become *Being and Nothingness*, to mention just two examples. A notable exception may be Karl Marx's *Das Kapital*, whose title literally translates into English as *The Capital*, which might have unintended connotations.

In films produced by the dominant Anglo-Saxon film industry, everyone speaks English, including foreigners, who usually speak their own varieties of broken English. German *Wehrmacht* officers speak English with a strong German accent, for example. Hercule Poirot, Agatha Christie's Belgian detective, was immortalized by Peter Ustinov, an English actor who was proficient in various languages and accents.

As Hercule Poirot, Ustinov spoke English with a thick French accent. And, of course, we shouldn't forget Manuel ('I am from Barcelona') in *Fawlty Towers*, played by another English actor, Andrew Sachs, who adopted a Spanish/Catalan accent. It doesn't really matter that your average German, Belgian, or Spaniard does not speak English like a *Wehrmacht* officer, Hercule Poirot, or Manuel from Barcelona – the use of the stereotype serves to make the character identifiable to the audience.

Adaptations of stories can go further than just language. The whole world knows the Walt Disney version of *Snow White*, and it's easy to forget that this and other fairy tales were first collected and popularized by the Brothers Grimm, nineteenth-century German linguists and lexicographers. Disney's Americanized version is a far cry from the version published by Jacob and Wilhelm Grimm, whose account is to be understood in the context of German nation-building.[13] The brothers' main interest was in collecting traditional folk stories, which they believed represented a pure form of national literature. They also believed that German unity, which was only achieved after their deaths, would rely on a full knowledge of cultural history. Disney's *Snow White* was released in a completely different era, shortly before the Second World War, and reflected Disney's anti-communist ideology. Disney's *Snow White* has even been interpreted as a virtual call to war, one which aims to re-establish the Old World order, represented by the seven dwarfs who have been given individual personalities and names, unlike in the Grimm version.[14]

English in business, politics, and education

English in business

English is used in everyday life all over the world. In cities as diverse as Atlanta, Bilbao, and Chengdu, for example, shopping malls are looking increasingly similar. English is there in advertisements, signs, and the names of brands and shops. It has become the language of global commerce and business. While English is dominant in multinational corporations, this is less the case in small, locally owned businesses.

Many companies all over the world have adopted English as their corporate language, even though they are based in non-English-speaking countries. This is even the case in France, with its policy of promoting French – food services company Sodexo, for example, uses English as its official language. Using English reduces translation costs, and quite often English is the only common language in companies operating worldwide. As a result, English is perceived as an *enabler* of efficient communication across geographies. Driven by economic and pragmatic arguments, companies such as Nissan in Japan implemented an English First strategy in the late 1990s. In the meantime, the policy has become English Only, a trend which has been followed by other companies from Japan (Honda) to Germany (Siemens). The English Only language policy may not apply to everyone in the company, but in general staff members are expected to know English. Lower-level employees, many of whom do not speak English, may receive communications in different languages, but this looks likely to change at some point too. Some multinational corporations, such as Honda in Japan, are pushing to make English the official language of the company by 2020.[15]

English may be the dominant language of business, but it is not used or prioritized everywhere. In Italy, for instance, only 29 per cent of people speak English, and in Brazil this number drops to 5 per cent.[16] Moreover, speaking one main language may sideline other cultures. Therefore, it is important not only to focus on English as a common language, but to develop intercultural competences as well. One of the alleged reasons why the merger between German BMW and British Rover failed was that the two sides interpreted cultural issues differently. For instance, shaking hands is far more common in Germany than in the UK.[17] Thus, something as simple as a handshake (or the absence of it) can have a major impact. Businesspeople from different countries speak English together as they do not expect to know each other's language. Yet the cultural differences between them may be underrated and even concealed by the use of English.

Another example of an inability to understand each other's language and culture is the merger between Dutch airline KLM and Air France.[18] Whereas the French have the impression that the Dutch are only interested in making a profit, the Dutch think that the French are attached to hierarchy and political interests which are not in the interest of the company. This 'clash of national cultures' threatens to make the company unmanageable. The interesting thing about these examples is that they involve countries which belong to the same Western civilization. Instead of the 'clash of civilizations' predicted by the American political scientist Samuel Huntington,[19] we may be witnessing clashes within a civilization. One might argue that a 'war' is being fought between cultures and languages rather than between countries or companies.

English in politics

English was introduced in the outer circle as a result of the British colonization of Africa and Asia. English became a crucial language in government, education, and law in East Africa (Kenya, Uganda, Tanzania, Malawi, Zambia, and Zimbabwe), where extensive British settlements were established, and it was also introduced in South Asia (India, Pakistan, Bangladesh, Sri Lanka, Nepal, and Bhutan). The increasing importance of English in the expanding circle is far more recent, and can be traced back to the growing importance of the United States after the First World War, when the United States entered the international arena.

For a long time, French remained the language of international politics and diplomacy. Even after the Battle of Waterloo in 1815, the language retained its status, despite France losing its status as a leading power to Britain. Similarly, after the 1870 war against Germany, in which France was crushed by its enemy, the peace treaty was written in French only. The hegemony of the French language was accepted by the British and the Germans. In 1919, however, at the peace conference after the First World War, US President Woodrow Wilson objected to the exclusive use of French and demanded equal status for English. British Prime Minister David Lloyd

George supported Wilson's move, emphasizing that there were far more speakers of English than of French in the world. There may be some irony in the fact that the French victory in the war marked the decline of their language in the world.

In today's international politics, English has replaced French as the leading language. This may be observed in political arenas such as international organizations and their assemblies. The United Nations recognizes six official languages, which also feature in the world's top ten languages: Arabic, Chinese, English, French, Russian, and Spanish. These are the languages that are used for the dissemination of official documents, and in which each representative of a country may speak. However, the six languages are not completely equal, as the Secretariat uses English and French as its working languages. Moreover, the United Nations has been criticized for relying too much on English only. German, the language of one of the major economies of the world but also of the instigator of two world wars, is not an official language. Japanese, which is similar to German in this respect, is not an official language either. Several other assemblies and parliaments around the world have similar multilingual practices. Currently, the European Parliament has 24 official languages, reflecting the official languages spoken in its member-states. In reality, these languages are not equal either. The list of the top five languages spoken during plenary sessions reveals that English is the preferred language, followed by German, French, Italian, and Spanish.[20] Although MPs can speak in their native language, many prefer to use English. In general, MPs from the north of Europe are more fluent in English than their colleagues from the south and the east, and younger MPs tend to speak it better than the older ones. To sum up, English may be called the unofficial language of international politics, and it is increasingly being used in assemblies and parliaments where speakers of different languages meet.

English in education

The diaspora of English has led to the development of New Englishes. This can cause considerable problems in an international educational context, as localized varieties of English are not always easily understood or accepted abroad. The problem is that most countries in the expanding circle (e.g. Europe) prefer and expect inner circle varieties of English (mainly British or American), while outer circle varieties are regarded as being somehow deficient. For example, students from India, some of whom have been educated entirely in English, often face problems with their English in an international academic context. The problem is that many of these people use a variety of English that is specific to their home country – a variety which reflects their first language rather than British or American English, something they may not even be aware of. To add insult to injury, they may find themselves being corrected by speakers of English from the inner circle or even the expanding circle, a situation which is likely to elicit sensitivities.

Higher education has become a lucrative business all over the world. Countries as diverse as China, Congo, and Cuba have all adopted measures to introduce English in their curricula as a means of gaining access to the world. Consequently,

British and American universities export their education in the form of language teachers, course materials, tests, methodologies, and ideologies. And they import large numbers of students who are willing to pay high entrance fees to study at their universities. The United States and the United Kingdom play host to the majority of the international student population, which mainly consists of students from Asia. One in five international students is Chinese.[21] International students are indispensable in today's higher education, which is characterized by marketization, privatization, and commodification. In an attempt to obtain their share of the cake, universities in non-English-speaking countries have followed suit and begun providing education in English as well. Higher education, and especially private education, has become a significant money-making venture, contributing to what may be called global academic capitalism.[22]

In spite of the globalization and internationalization of education, language testing is still very much organized according to 'national' boundaries, and test-taking institutions protect their own markets. A good example is the Association of Language Testers in Europe (ALTE), which explicitly stipulates that its members can only provide examinations of the official language(s) spoken in their own countries, meaning English language tests can only be developed by English-speaking countries.[23] This, of course, runs counter to the idea of English as a truly common language, no longer owned by a particular country. The best-known English language tests are the Test of English as a Foreign Language (TOEFL), launched in 1964 by a private American non-profit organization, and the International English Language Testing System (IELTS), which was launched in 1980 by the British Council and the University of Cambridge English Language Assessment. Both are high-stakes tests taken for migration or study purposes in English-speaking countries. The dominance of these two tests reflects the pressure to subscribe to either British or American standard varieties of English and the ideology of the inherent superiority of native speaker English.[24]

Apart from testing and teaching practices, English has the upper hand in publications as well. The phrase 'publish or perish' might better be rephrased 'publish in English or perish', as it is only publications in English that really count. This explains why many journals have become English-only publications, even though some of them have retained their original names (e.g. *Association Internationale de Linguistique Appliquée*, AILA).[25] Several books won international acclaim only after they had been translated into English. Other books caught world attention as they were published in English only. A good example may be *Language and Symbolic Power* by the French sociologist Pierre Bourdieu, which does not have a direct counterpart in French. If a book or an article is not written in English, it does not seem to exist.

Whereas teaching and learning in English have been firmly established in the outer circle, this is a fairly recent trend in the expanding circle. The increasing importance of English in European higher education can be traced back to the Bologna Process, named after the 1999 Bologna Declaration, whose main aim was to create a European Higher Education Area. The irony is that although Bologna aimed to promote the diversity of languages and cultures in Europe, the process actually led to more English. Universities want to attract students and lecturers from other countries, but they can only do this successfully if they provide education in English. Moreover, universities are increasingly organized as corporations and they want to cash in on foreign students. Students thus become customers in an increasingly competitive market, and they prefer to 'go shopping' in places where they can study in English. As a consequence of all this, the internationalization of higher education has led to its marketization and commodification. English has played a crucial role in this process..

While English-medium instruction is on the rise all over Europe, it is more common in the north of the continent than in the south. Universities in the Nordic countries (in particular Finland) are at the forefront in the process of *Englishization*, together with universities in the Netherlands. It should be noted that most languages spoken in the north of Europe are related to English (Finnish being the exception), which makes it somewhat easier for their speakers to study and teach in English. Furthermore, these countries have been exposed to English – their second language – for many years, whereas countries in the south of the continent were more oriented towards French, the language they are related to and which they used as a second language. Countries in the east of Europe were historically exposed to German and in more recent history to Russian. It was only after the fall of communism that English began to seep into these countries. Last but not least, the languages spoken in the north and east of Europe are not world languages, unlike some of the languages spoken in the south (such as French, Spanish, and Portuguese). They therefore need English to gain access to the world.[26]

The use of English in higher education is not undisputed in Europe. Even in countries which are generally considered to be pro-English (such as the Netherlands), concerns have been raised over the quality and the necessity of education in English in a non-English-speaking context. The Royal Netherlands Academy of Arts and Sciences, an advisory body to the Dutch government, argued in favour of Dutch as the default language and English as an optional language in higher education.[27] In reality, however, it is almost the other way round: English has become dominant at Dutch universities, especially at graduate level, while Dutch is not even an option in many cases. At the same time, there have been many complaints about the poor level of English (of students as well as lecturers) and about the fact that Dutch students cannot study in their own language anymore. Until now, however, these complaints have been gleefully neglected.

The main arguments against the excessive use of English in higher education can be summarized as follows. First, English can lead to social exclusion as not all groups in society have the same access to English, not even in affluent countries such as the Netherlands. For most students, learning in a second language is a particular challenge, and for many it is already difficult to cope with their first language of education (e.g. Dutch). Recent research has pointed out that students' linguistic skills in the first language tend to be worryingly low. Second, in a professional context, most students will need the national or regional language rather than

English, except when they work in an international context. Therefore, good education in the local language is a prerequisite. Third, there will be domain loss for the national language, which was standardized in the nineteenth century and since then has developed into a full-fledged academic language with its own traditions, terminology, and so on. There are fears that English is becoming the new Latin and that the national language may return to its status of a vernacular. Last but not least, the identity discourse establishes strong links between language and identity. This discourse is prevalent in right-wing rhetoric, which is on the rise all over Europe.

Apart from teaching and learning purposes, English is also increasingly used as a language of internal and external communication, often in combination with the local language. Unfortunately, this does not necessarily lead to better communication. In an email sent to all users at a European university whose name I will not disclose here, the message was conveyed that there were pickpockets on the campus. Unfortunately, in the English version of the message the word *sniper* was used instead of *pickpocket*. Even though the mistake was rectified in a follow-up message, the message caused considerable panic among those who could not read the accompanying message in the local language. The example shows that messages can get lost in translation, and that poor translations can lead to Babylonian chaos.

In many countries all over the world, learning English often starts in kindergarten or earlier, and children may be familiar with *Snow White* (most probably in the Disney version) before they know stories from their own cultures. This may seem regrettable, but it is very much part of today's globalizing culture. English is taught in primary and secondary schools worldwide, and it is commonly regarded as a prerequisite for academic success. As reported in *China Daily*, more than 70 per cent of Chinese parents want their children to learn English to help them get into better schools and thus improve their chances in life.[28] The global success of English is not due to the inherent qualities of the language, but to the fact that it can empower people in all walks of life. However, access to good education (often private education) is usually restricted to those who can afford high tuition fees.

Notes

1 Acemoglu and Robinson (2013).
2 Galeano (1971/1997).
3 This is known as the Muhlenberg legend, after Frederick Muhlenberg, the first Speaker of the US House of Representatives.
4 Kachru (1985).
5 Kachru (1985).
6 Kachru (2005). See also Schneider (2007).
7 Vertovec (2007), Blommaert (2010).
8 Widdowson (1994).
9 Jenkins (2009).
10 Edwards (2016).
11 See: www.weforum.org/agenda/2015/11/the-20-most-influential-books-in-history/ (accessed 2 January 2019).
12 Crystal (2003).

13 Bauman and Briggs (2003: 197–225).
14 See: www.popten.net/2008/06/the-moral-of-snow-white/ (accessed 4 August 2017).
15 See: www.bbc.com/capital/story/20180808-what-is-the-future-of-english-in-the-us?ocid=ww.social.link.email (accessed 28 August 2018).
16 See: www.bbc.com/capital/story/20170317-the-international-companies-using-only-english (accessed 3 August 2017).
17 Boye (2016). See: http://waxmann.ciando.com/img/books/extract/383098409X_lp.pdf (accessed 3 January 2018).
18 See: www.theguardian.com/business/2017/jul/20/french-dutch-culture-clash-revealed-leaked-air-france-klm-report (accessed 5 March 2019).
19 Huntington (1996).
20 See: www.theguardian.com/education/datablog/2014/may/21/european-parliament-english-language-official-debates-data (accessed 20 August 2017).
21 Yu and Moskal (2019).
22 Gill and Kirkpatrick (2013).
23 The 2018 ALTE Constitution states that 'Each Member shall provide examinations of the official language or languages which is/are spoken in their own country or region' (Article 1). Available at: https://nl.alte.org/resources/Documents/ALTE%20Constitution%20Revised%20April%202018.pdf (accessed 4 January 2019).
24 Tupas and Salonga (2016).
25 See: www.uia.org/s/or/en/1100046643 (accessed 3 January 2019).
26 Wächter and Maiworm (2014).
27 See: https://knaw.nl/en/news/news/language-choice-in-higher-education-demands-custom-approach (accessed 28 May 2019).
28 See: www.chinadaily.com.cn/beijing/2013-11/14/content_17112871.htm (accessed 3 January 2019).

7
LANGUAGE AND WAR

The war of words

Conflicts over languages can turn into violent clashes, even wars. Again, there is a link between language and politics, and war. As Carl von Clausewitz, the Prussian general and military theorist, famously explained, 'war is the continuation of politics with other means'.[1] While the concept of a language war can be taken literally, it is often used in a metaphorical sense. A metaphor is a figure of speech in which a word or phrase is applied to an object or action to which it is not literally applicable. In the metaphor 'language war', language is seen as some kind of fight, even though no real fighting is taking place. As Lakoff and Johnson point out in their seminal study *Metaphors We Live By*, metaphors are pervasive in everyday life.[2] That is, people construct meaning as they think in metaphors. Metaphors are a means to conceptualize the world, and metaphorical language usually expresses a hidden ideology. For instance, if one refers to the *tsunami* of English, it is quite likely that one believes English will 'flood' all other languages, which as a consequence are destined to 'drown'.

Metaphors of violence and war are salient when it comes to linguistic and cultural identities, as language is often associated with power relations, conflict, struggle, and threat. It may be no surprise that narratives often refer to a glorious past or a heroic battle. A good example is the Battle of Kosovo (15 June 1389) between the Serbs and the invading Ottoman Empire, in which Serbia was defeated.[3] It is almost impossible to reconstruct what happened exactly, as there are few reliable historical accounts of the battle, and the warring factions and their allies developed different narratives. Therefore, the Battle of Kosovo can also be understood as a *battle of narratives*. Moreover, the battle serves as an important *lieu de mémoire*[4] for Serbian national identity, which came to symbolize the long struggle for national statehood, as a result of which the battle entered the collective Serbian memory.

In 1989, on the 600th anniversary of the Battle of Kosovo, Serbian leader Slobodan Milošević delivered an infamous speech on the site of the battle, which has been described as a forecast of Yugoslavia's collapse and the bloodshed of the ensuing wars.[5] In his 15-minutes speech, addressing an estimated 1 million cheering crowd, Milošević describes the Battle of Kosovo as a heroic event in which the Serbs' lack of unity and betrayal led to their defeat and humiliation, a fate for which they suffered for a full six centuries. Now it is time for new battles, Milošević argues. Even though Milošević appears to refer to the word 'battle' in a metaphorical sense, he does not exclude an armed conflict. To which he adds the cautionary words, 'regardless of what kind of battles they are, they cannot be won without resolve, bravery, and sacrifice, without the noble qualities that were present here in the field of Kosovo in the days past.'[6] In his speech, Milošević describes the Serbs as a great, brave, and proud people who have never exploited other people. On the contrary, they have been oppressed and endangered by 'the others', a threat which has been hanging like a sword over their heads.

The Western media stressed Milošević's appalling display of Serbian nationalist rhetoric and his glorification of the Serbian imagined community. According to the Serbian point of view, Western media highlighted anti-Serbian narratives and they reduced a complex reality to the focus on a 'brutal leader' and an 'evil people'. In this view, Milošević's 'tolerant speech' has been deliberately misinterpreted and mistranslated as an incitement to genocide.[7] Anyway, the example illustrates how the past is often used (or abused) to justify actions taken in the present and even in the future.

Words played an important role in the ensuing Yugoslav Wars (1991–2001), a series of separate but related conflicts in which ethnic, religious, political, and linguistic fault lines overlapped, and in which the warring factions constructed their own narratives, framing the war in entirely different ways. Most Serbs, the largest nation in Yugoslavia, favoured the country remaining intact, and they saw the rise of nationalism in the other republics as a threat to Yugoslav unity. The other nations saw Yugoslavia as being dominated by the Serbs, whom they regarded as intolerant and brutal. The latter image was also disseminated in the Western media. Even today, more than 20 years after the war, the wounds have not healed. One may see road signs on which the Cyrillic script has been erased as it is commonly associated with the Serbs and their Russian allies.

As pointed out earlier, the use of a particular script or spelling can play an important role in the construction of one's identity. The same applies to words. Perhaps the most telling example is the euphemism 'ethnic cleansing' (as it came to be known in English), which was used by the perpetrators of war crimes to refer to the forced removal of ethnic groups from the territory they claimed as theirs in order to create homogeneous ethnic regions. The removal of large groups of people often resulted in their extermination. The term 'ethnic cleansing' is reminiscent to the 'final solution', the Nazi genocide of the Jews during the Second World War. What these terms have in common is that they use words with positive

FIGURE 7.1 Road sign in Bosnia and Herzegovina: Oborci/Оборци
Source: Ann Peckstadt

connotations (clean/cleanse, solution) to cover up the most atrocious war crimes. They make acceptable what is not acceptable.

During and after the war in the Balkans, new identities were created. New borders were drawn, and new flags, passports, and currencies were introduced, to mention just a few measures to stress the differences between the new nations. Also, the language was made different, and the war of words continued. On the motorway between Belgrade and Zagreb, for instance, Serbs and Croats introduced different words for toll, which is now called *putarina* in Serbia and *cestarina* in Croatia, even though both words existed in Serbo-Croatian. The breakdown of language can also be observed in ordinary words such as coffee, which is now called *kava* in Croatia and *kafa* in Serbia (written кафа in Cyrillic, which makes the words look even more different). In Croatia, many new words have been created to 'purify' the language from foreign influences. For instance, the word *kontejner*, a Slavicized word derived from container, is now referred to as *smećnjak* (from Serbo-Croatian *smeće*, trash). In Serbia, many old words derived from religion are entering the language. On the other hand, young people often use words derived from English (e.g. *kulirati*: to be cool). Bosnian Muslims have adopted many words from Arabic and Turkish, for instance for religious festivities. Like in Turkish, they say *merhaba* when greeting people. As the regions have become different countries, their languages are growing apart too. Yet this is not a natural phenomenon, but a carefully orchestrated political manoeuvre.

82 Language is politics

It is key to remember that these communities, while fundamentally sharing the same language, were under different spheres of cultural influence for centuries. Moreover, many linguistic differences are far older than most recent changes: many words in Croat were appropriated from the German- or Italian-speaking spheres while the influences in Serbian were Russian and Greek.

Last but not least, it should be noted that Kosovo is called Kosova (mind the important one letter-difference) by the ethnic Albanian majority in the region, which declared its independence from Serbia in 2008. However, Serbia does not recognize Kosovo as an independent state, while internationally it is a 'partially recognized state' and thus remains a disputed area to the current day.[8] Kosovo is the commonly accepted name in English, while pro-independence supporters use the name Kosova. The name of the 'blackbird field' (*Kosovo Polje* in Serbian, *Fushë Kosovë* in Albanian), where the 1389 battle took place, was applied to the province created in 1864. From a linguistic point of view, Kosovo stands apart from the other nations in former Yugoslavia: Albanian (a language Kosovo shares with neighbouring Albania) is as different from Serbian as English is from Welsh. Therefore, the Albanian language serves as an important marker of identity in Kosovo.[9]

Of course former Yugoslavia is not the only region in the world where language has been exploited to the benefit of competing factions. Another example of a war in which words play a crucial role is Egypt, which after its revolution (or coup, depending on one's interpretation) experienced another war: a battle for language.[10] Since 2011, the country's many factions have been imposing their own narratives on events. Amira Hanafi, an Egyptian-American artist fascinated by this linguistic battle, interviewed hundreds of Egyptians to find out what the words commonly used in the revolution/coup mean to them. Her *Dictionary of the Revolution*,[11] which comes in Arabic as well as English, is freely available on the internet. It consists of 160 words and concepts related to the events which took place in Egypt. The words are presented in a diagram revealing the links between the words, and each word relates to a story which you can read if you click on the word. One of the words is Tahrir Square, a place in downtown Cairo and the location for political demonstrations. In addition, Tahrir Square is a *lieu de mémoire* and a strong metaphor which stands for freedom. One of the central parts in the story illustrates this very clearly: 'Tahrir Square is where we first started to taste freedom. The name Tahrir Square will forever be the square of freedom'. Later in the text, there is another reference to Tahrir which somehow contradicts the idea of the square as a symbol of freedom: 'Now [Tahrir Square] is almost a military institution or something like that, because of the walls. Everywhere we go there are walls and barbed wire. There isn't one open place in Tahrir Square'.

Amira Hanafi refers to her dictionary as a 'polyvocal history'. That is, she sees it as a document of a dialogue between herself and a plurality of other voices, which is informed by the participants' own experiences and interpretations. As a consequence, the dictionary and indeed the whole project find their limits in time. In today's Egypt, Tahrir could stand for completely different images (e.g. freedom gone wrong). In *A Dictionary of the Revolution*, meanings are not fixed and they reflect a myriad of opinions, not just the artist's. Therefore, the project is called *a* dictionary, not *the* dictionary. It should be seen as a form of history-telling in which history can be understood as multiple and non-linear, and continually negotiated.[12] It goes without saying that Hanafi's conceptualization of a dictionary is very different from the traditional concept, in which meanings are fixed and attributed from the lexicographer's perspective.

As the examples of former Yugoslavia and Egypt show, the groups involved in a language war or any other conflict are typically referred to by means of stereotyped images. Whereas the in-group ('we') is constructed as the oppressed, the out-group ('they') is seen as the oppressor. The in-group imagines itself as a victim or underdog which is threatened by an enemy against whom protection is sought or action should be taken. A language war can be described as a fight in which the oppressed struggle to defend their language and narratives against the oppressor. Words play a crucial part in this war. For instance, what is regarded as a liberation by one group may be an occupation for another group. A good example is Tibet, which, according to the Chinese, was *liberated* by them in 1959, whereas Tibet and the Western world see it as an *occupation*. Similarly, the US *embargo* of Cuba is called a *blockade* (*el bloqueo*) in Cuba. This different framing and the use of metaphorical language affect the way in which reality is perceived and interpreted.

FIGURE 7.2 Tahrir Square during the revolution/coup (the banner reads 'The People Want the Downfall of the Regime')
Source: Ruth Vandewalle

The killing fields of language

The oppression of a language and its speakers can culminate in a real fight and even in a full-scale war. Any language can be a threat to another language and any language can be a threatened language. An oppressed language can develop into an oppressor, depending on the context. Violence may erupt over anything related to language. People have been threatened, humiliated, maimed, or even killed for speaking their own language or for not speaking the language of their oppressor. Before the US Civil War (1861–1865), slave owners were reported to cut out the tongues of slaves unable or unwilling to speak English. During the war, Francophones were executed to discourage the use of French. In subsequent decades, Blackfoot Indians were beaten if they spoke their native language. The list of examples is endless.[13]

During the era of nation-building in Europe, France forcefully introduced its language all over the French nation and its newly conquered territories in and outside Europe. The languages of the conquered areas were ruthlessly suppressed, as a result of which the nation was entirely Frenchified. In France, hardly any traces are left of these minority languages, which were wiped out on purpose. In their colonies, the French pursued the same policies. In Algeria, for instance, they banned Arabic at primary school, dismissing it as a backward language. In today's world, however, France feels dominated by English and measures have been taken to protect French. The example shows that the oppressor may become the oppressed, and vice versa, depending on the context and shifting power relations in particular. Of course, France is not the only assailant turned victim. The same happened in Spain, another former empire, which suppressed its own minority languages as well as the indigenous languages in its colonies in Latin America. During the Franco dictatorship, speakers of languages other than Castilian Spanish were humiliated, fined, and taken to jail. Minority languages such as Basque (Euskara) were meant to disappear. Today, Spain too feels threatened by English, and similar measures as in France have been taken to protect Spanish. Ironically, minority languages are protected too, after they had almost been wiped out.

The same strategies may be observed in other parts of the world as well. The Kurds in Syria, who have been denied basic rights for decades, were banned from speaking and teaching their own language. In Turkey, the Kurds were even referred to as 'Mountain Turks' in an effort to cover up their identity and language. In Hong Kong (and across the South China region in general), Cantonese is being suppressed as a first language due to China's efforts to promote Mandarin as the unifying language. The *Hindustan Times* reported on protests over the imposition of Hindu signages in a Kannada-speaking area, following earlier clashes in which trucks were set on fire.[14] A myriad of other examples could be cited.

Not only are people being killed, but their cultural heritage is attacked as well. Books and libraries are destroyed to kill ideas as well as the language in which these ideas are expressed. A plaque at the entrance of the former library in Sarajevo commemorates the night of 25–26 August 1992, when the building, the national and university library of Bosnia and Herzegovina, was set on fire. More than 2 million books and documents vanished in the flames. The plaque, which condemns the 'Serbian criminals' for the atrocities committed during the war in the Balkans, is meant as a reminder and a warning. In the meantime, the building stands again. Although no longer a library, the building has been meticulously restored with the help of Western countries, revealing political alliances as well as the conviction that ideas cannot be killed.

In most language conflicts, the majority imposes its language on the minority. In some cases, a powerful minority can also impose its language on a powerless majority. The latter was the case in nineteenth-century Belgium, a country known for its language divide which has been pulling the country apart for decades. Although the 'language struggle' led to some violent conflicts in the past, it never ended in civil war as in former Yugoslavia. Yet it appears that Belgium is slowly falling apart, a process which has been institutionalized in a series of complex state reforms, based on the linguistic division of the country. The conflict is framed in powerful metaphors in which language is commonly associated with war (hence also the concept of language struggle). Although the linguistic tensions may be more severe in Belgium than in other bi- or multilingual countries (e.g. Switzerland), Belgium is by no means unique. The fault lines tearing the country apart may be observed in other countries as well. Belgium is a good example of nineteenth-century

FIGURE 7.3 Sarajevo library
Source: Frank van Splunder

European power politics, and today it is a complex multilingual country in the heart of Europe. In the next paragraphs, the Belgian language situation will be discussed in some more detail. First of all, let's have a look at the historical context to put things in perspective.[15]

Belgium could be called a British invention. After Napoleon's defeat in 1815, Europe's rulers met in Vienna to redraw the national boundaries of the continent. The Low Countries, roughly today's Belgium and the Netherlands, were reunited in the newly established Kingdom of the Netherlands. The purpose was to create a strong buffer state against France, but the new state turned out to be too strong, challenging the equilibrium in Europe. The Belgian Revolution against the Dutch in 1830 was welcomed (and perhaps instigated) by the main European powers, who sought to gain influence in the new kingdom. The first king, Leopold I, was the British-backed candidate for the Belgian crown, but as a German prince who had fought against Napoleon in the Imperial Russian Army, he was also acceptable for the other victors of the war. After Napoleon's defeat, Leopold moved to the United Kingdom, where he married Princess Charlotte of Wales, the daughter of the future King George IV. After a year of marriage, Charlotte died in childbirth, but Leopold remained in the United Kingdom, where he enjoyed considerable status. The Belgian king Leopold I was Queen Victoria's uncle, whose marriage with his nephew Albert he arranged in 1840. Leopold was fluent in German, his native language, as well as French, the international language of prestige, and English, the language of his adopted country. Interestingly, the name of his kingdom, Belgium, is the old name used for the Netherlands in the humanist period, which in its turn refers to the tribe of the *Belgae* in the time of the Romans. Thus, a great past was imagined for the new country, which was created less than 200 years ago.

In the 1830s, the north of Belgium (Dutch-speaking Flanders) was poor and the south (French-speaking Wallonia) was rich. In reality, most people did not speak the standardized variety of their language, but only their local dialect, in Flanders as well as in Wallonia. In other countries, this was very much the same situation. Belgium was created as a French-speaking country, even though French was the language of the minority. Yet it was the language of a powerful minority which dominated the country in all respects. Dutch, the language of the majority in Belgium, was disdainfully regarded as merely a number of dialects. Moreover, it was called Flemish rather than Dutch to make it look different from the language spoken in the Netherlands, and possibly to prevent the secession of Flanders.[16] In order to achieve any status in the country (or upward social mobility, as it is called), one had to know French, the only language of prestige in Belgium. As a consequence, Flemings had to be bilingual, whereas the French-speakers were monolingual. All important positions in the country were given to monolingual speakers of French, even in Flanders. After a long and bitter battle for equal rights, Dutch was accepted as an official language in 1898, even though in practice it was far from equal with French. Much later, the struggle for linguistic rights gradually developed into a movement for political and economic rights.

The emancipation of Flanders took almost 100 years, when a Flemish elite gradually emerged. Although this university-educated generation, which was born around the early 1900s, had studied entirely in French, they were the main supporters of education in Dutch, their native language. Several of these people, generally of modest descent, were trained as medical doctors or other professions, and became active in politics, often as Flemish nationalists. The Flemings realised the importance of instruction in their own language in order to create a Flemish elite and to gain power in the country. All efforts to set up higher education in Dutch were met by staunch resistance by the French-speaking authorities who rejected the use of Dutch as a language of education. The Catholic Church and the leading clergy in particular argued that Dutch was unfit as a medium of instruction, even though Dutch had proved to be successful in the Netherlands. In 1917, during the First World War, the German occupier met Flemish demands to set up a Dutch-language university so as to create goodwill for their own policies. This proved to be disastrous, as after the war the decision was overturned and French remained the language of higher education in Flanders. It was not until 1932 that Ghent University adopted Dutch as its medium of instruction, even though the decision was heavily contested by the French-speaking elite.

In a series of complex state reforms from the 1960s onwards, Belgium was gradually transformed into a federal state, based on communities (linked to language) and regions (linked to territory). Today's Belgium has three official languages (Dutch, French, German), each of which is linked to a particular community and region: Dutch is the official language in Flanders (bordering the Netherlands), French in Wallonia (bordering France), and German in the Eastern Cantons (bordering Germany). In Brussels, French and Dutch are both official, even though French is clearly dominant. The language regulations are very strict, and they may remind one of some kind of self-imposed apartheid. The reforms seek to compromise entirely different narratives and conceptualizations of the state. Whereas the Flemings are generally in favour of more autonomy or even independence, the French-speaking part of the country tries to preserve the unity and the status quo. The pull towards more autonomy is particularly strong in Flanders, since the moderate Flemish nationalists emerged as the largest political party and dominant force in the country.

Since the 1970s, Flanders has become the richest region in Belgium, whereas the south is suffering from an ailing economy. Today, the south feels dominated by the north, much in the same way as the north felt dominated by the south 100 years ago. It should be noted that the present division of languages does not reflect the multilingual reality in today's Belgium. Due to migration since the 1960s, many other languages, cultures, and religions have been brought to the country. In certain urban areas, Dutch as well as French have become de facto minority languages, and English is increasingly being used as a lingua franca. Like many other European countries, Belgium has become a multicultural and multilingual society, as a result of which new tensions and fault lines have emerged. As a consequence, far-right Flemish nationalism changed its focus: in its narratives, the French-speaking dominant class, which has lost most of its power anyway, has been replaced by Islam as the main threat to one's native culture. The same tendency may be observed all over Europe, where anti-immigration populist parties have emerged as well.[17]

Although Finland is very different from Belgium, there are some striking similarities as well.[18] As in Flanders, language played a crucial role as a nation-building tool in nineteenth-century Finland. Moreover, the majority language (Finnish) was actually dominated by the minority language (Swedish), and the language struggle was exploited by outsiders (Russia). In contrast to Belgium, both linguistic groups supported the national cause.

Finland was a part of Sweden from the twelfth until the early nineteenth century, a legacy reflected in the prevalence of Swedish as an official language in Finland.[19] Swedish became the dominant language of the nobility, administration, and education in the seventeenth century, while Finnish was the language of the peasantry, clergy, and local courts. As a result, the educated class was almost entirely Swedish-speaking. While the majority's language lacked prestige and was commonly seen as a peasant language, the minority's language was associated with high culture and education. Swedish was a prerequisite for social and educational advancement in Finland and higher education was entirely in Swedish. As a result, Finland only narrowly escaped *Swedishization* much in the same way as Flanders escaped *Frenchification*.[20]

The Finnish language struggle, which was embedded in the Romantic nationalist movement, eventually led to the gradual recognition of the majority language in domains which for a very long time had been reserved for the minority language. Like in Belgium, the language struggle was exploited by a foreign country to support its own cause. When Sweden ceded Finland to Russia in 1809 after they had lost the Finnish War, Finland became an autonomous grand duchy within the Russian Empire. The tsar made Finnish equal to Swedish in an attempt to weaken the influence of the Swedish elite. Later on, the policy of *Russification* aimed to increase the use of Russian in Finland. Finnish as well as many Swedish-speaking Finns, who were cut off from Sweden, were in favour of the national Finnish cause as they feared Russian domination. The Russian Revolution prompted the Finnish Declaration of Independence in 1917. Interestingly, Flanders declared its independence in the same year, but it was stillborn. In today's Finland, Finnish has attained a dominant status and the language issue has lost its inflammability.[21]

The tsunami of English

In today's world, English is the usual suspect. Even though the use of English is embraced in many parts of the world, English is also portrayed as a 'killer language' which gains from the extinction of other languages. Metaphorically, the language is referred to as a Tyrannosaurus rex, the ultimate predator.[22] In one of the interviews I conducted, English was described as a tsunami, a tremendous force that swipes away all other languages. In narratives which perceive English as a threat to other languages, the language is typically associated with violence (natural or physical) and war. The English language is framed as the oppressor and the other languages as the oppressed. The struggle against the expansion of English may be linked to various ideological perspectives. Whereas a right-wing nationalist perspective puts the emphasis on the protection of one's own language, culture, and identity, a left-wing perspective stresses its democratic or anti-capitalist and anti-imperialist motivation. The dominance of English has been referred to as *linguistic imperialism*, which is also the title of a book published almost 30 years ago in which the author, Robert Phillipson, condemns the role of English in the world and its devastating effect on other languages. Phillipson, who argues in favour of linguistic human rights, targets the way English language learning has been promoted all over the world. Phillipson is particularly critical about the role of institutions such as the British Council, which he accuses of commerce-driven state interference in language matters.[23]

There may be some irony in the fact that English is not an official language in either the United Kingdom or the United States, the core countries of the *inner circle* of English. Although English was never imposed as the official language of the United States, it gradually became the dominant language. Unlike France, in which the French language is protected by law, there is no similar language legislation in the United States. Even though several states have passed laws to make English the official language, its de facto dominance is not laid down in federal legislation. This may be due to the fact that most Americans (and Anglophones in general) do not have the same allegiances to their language as Francophones. As observed earlier, English-speaking countries tend to shy away from language legislation. On the other hand, American attitudes towards languages have changed in the last centuries and even decades. In the early colonial period, a number of languages competed with English: in the eighteenth and nineteenth centuries, Dutch, Swedish, and German were widely spoken in the colonies which later became the United States of America, while Spanish and French were predominant outside those colonies. After the First World War, an ideological shift took place. This shift was caused by the hatred towards German-Americans, who were associated with the German enemy during the war, as well as distrust of the new Southern and Eastern European immigrants. From predominantly European immigration, the United States witnessed Latin American and Asian flows of immigrants. The early 1980s saw a rise in *nativism* (i.e. the policy of protecting the interests of native inhabitants against those of immigrants). This nativism was due to an increase in the number of minority language speakers, in particular those from the Spanish-speaking world. Spanish is increasingly spoken in the United States and therefore initiatives were taken to make English the official language, resulting in the development of the English Only movement, which is also known as the Official English movement.[24] Typically, proponents of this movement use the term 'Official English' and opponents call it 'English Only'. Self-proclaimed 'citizens' action groups' such as US English, English First, and ProEnglish have been set up to support their cause. Their goals are to gather and disseminate evidence to support the claim that most Americans want Official English (attempting to influence public opinion) and lobby Congress for Official English legislation, which is often about restricting immigrants' rights.

In contrast to the narratives in which English is perceived as a threat to other languages, the English Only movement frames English as threatened by other languages, in particular Spanish. As the name English Only suggests, the movement aims to restrict the use of languages other than English. While English is seen as a unifying force, other languages and multilingualism are thought to be destructive of national unity. In their narratives, Belgium is referred to as the ultimate disaster of what can happen if a country has more than one language. English Only claims that national unity, American identity, and the English language are threatened by immigration and languages other than English. Measures have been proposed to restrict bilingual education for language minority children, to limit linguistic access to political and civil rights, and to declare English the sole official language of the United States. According to Sam Pimm, the executive director of ProEnglish,[25] English Only would help immigrants better assimilate into American culture. He also argues that it could save the country billions of dollars in translation costs. In an effort to ward off claims of discrimination, Pimm claimed to help people achieve the American dream. In spite of these efforts to link English Only to social or emancipatory concerns, it is quite obvious that this is only a sham. The movement is mainly supported by conservative voters who feel threatened by other languages and cultures. Many leading Republicans support English Only, including current vice president Mike Pence. During the 2016 presidential election, Trump supporters made it quite obvious what the movement stands for: 'If you don't speak English, get out'. The message was conveyed on a picture with the American flag and the additional text 'This is America'.

Last but not least, it should be added that many Americans are monolingual speakers of English. The number of Americans learning other languages is low, and the United States is way behind most European countries in terms of learning foreign languages.[26] This may come as a surprise for a country essentially made up of immigrants. Yet many descendants of immigrant families are unable to speak their family's language of heritage. The language loss is often completed by the third generation. Some of the reasons of language loss will be discussed in the next chapter. Although recent waves of US nationalism and English Only rhetoric may give the impression that Americans are proud of their monolingualism, it remains a question how they can cope with English Only in a society which is becoming increasingly multicultural and multilingual.

Notes

1 von Clausewitz (1832, 1989). The original in German reads, '*Der Krieg ist eine bloße Fortsetzung der Politik mit anderen Mitteln*'.
2 Lakoff and Johnson (1980: 3).
3 Glenny (1996: 34). According to other sources, both armies were annihilated.
4 The concept of *lieu de mémoire* was popularized by the French historian Pierre Norda (1996).
5 Glenny (1996: 34–35).

6 The speech can be watched at: www.youtube.com/watch?v=td2SReWxogY&gl=BE (accessed 8 October 2019) (with subtitles in English). The English translation of the speech is available at: www.slobodan-milosevic.org/spch-kosovo1989.htm (accessed 12 February 2019).
7 See: www.hirhome.com/yugo/milospeech.htm (accessed 12 February 2019).
8 In order to be become a member of the United Nations, a state has to be recognized by two-thirds of the world's countries. See: www.un.org/en/sections/member-states/about-un-membership/index.html (accessed 25 March 2019).
9 Malcolm (1998).
10 See: www.theguardian.com/world/2014/jul/18/egypt-battle-for-language-dictionary-revolution-amira-hanafi (accessed 6 December 2018).
11 See: http://qamosalthawra.com/en (accessed 4 January 2019).
12 Amira Hanafi, personal communication, 14 February 2019.
13 Lake (2002). See: www.harvardmagazine.com/2002/03/language-wars.html (accessed 4 January 2019).
14 See:www.hindustantimes.com/india-news/language-war-pro-kannada-activists-to-team-up-with-dmk-to-protest-imposition-of-hindi/story-pdlQdBwhYPLsDlsBlWihVI.html (accessed 4 January 2019).
15 For a good survey of the language situation in Belgium, see Witte and Van Velthoven (1999).
16 Dalby (2002: 117).
17 Mudde (2007).
18 Van Splunder (2016).
19 Kirby (2006).
20 *Swedishization* of Finland: Coleman (2010). *Frenchification* of Flanders: Witte and Van Velthoven (1999).
21 Saarinen (2012).
22 Swales (1997).
23 Phillipson (1992: 138).
24 Lawton (2013).
25 See: https://proenglish.org (accessed 4 January 2019).
26 See: www.bbc.com/capital/story/20180808-what-is-the-future-of-english-in-the-us?ocid=ww.social.link.email (accessed 30 January 2019).

8
LIFE AND DEATH OF LANGUAGES

The struggle for life

In *The Origin of Species*, Charles Darwin describes the process of natural selection: species which are best adapted to their environment survive and reproduce, whereas those which are less adapted die out. This process ensures that only the fittest (i.e. those which are best adapted) survive to pass on their genes to the next generation. Darwin's theory of evolution was a revolutionary idea in the nineteenth century: in contrast to what was commonly believed in those days, Darwin showed that species were not separately created. In fact, they were not created at all. The logical consequence of the theory of evolution was that a Creator (or God) was no longer necessary to explain the world. Yet this is not what Darwin says. In the last chapter of his book, there is a very curious sentence in which the author refers to 'the laws impressed on matter by the Creator',[1] a passage that seems to contradict the very idea of evolution which he had developed in the preceding 400 pages. Much has been said about this reference to the Creator, but it seems plausible Darwin inserted the sentence in order not to be accused of atheism (even though most probably he was not an atheist himself). One should realize that in Darwin's times, Christianity was the dominant ideology in the Western world and the Church was still all-powerful. As a result, the idea of a world without God was simply unacceptable. Today, almost 200 years after its first publication, the theory of evolution has been widely accepted and secularism has become the dominant ideology, at least in many Western countries.

Although *The Origin of Species* is not a book about language, the ideas about evolution have been applied to language as well. That is, languages have often been regarded as organisms that 'are born, live, decay, and die' just like words do. The struggle for life, a concept introduced by Darwin, is a strong metaphor to describe this process. Perhaps an even stronger metaphor is the 'survival of the fittest', a phrase coined not by Charles Darwin, but by his contemporary Herbert Spencer.[2] The phrase refers to the process of natural selection and the ability of organisms to adapt. Unfortunately, its meaning is widely misunderstood as it is often interpreted as meaning unrestrained competition.

In many writings of the nineteenth century, it was common to speak of the 'life of languages', reflecting the biological model which had been introduced by Darwin's theory of evolution. Like living organisms, it was believed that languages were born and died, and new languages evolved as a result of the struggle for life and the survival of the fittest. Curiously, language change was often seen as a process of degeneration, which could only be restored by efforts to remodel or purify the language. In the industrial era, the biological model and its metaphors were replaced by a model which saw language as a tool or an instrument of communication. Today, we see language as a medium (e.g. a medium of instruction), even though the biological and industrial metaphors are still widely used.[3] As observed earlier, languages are often compared with natural forces such as an avalanche, a waterfall, and even a tsunami.

Language birth

The birth and death of a language are to be taken metaphorically, as there is no particular point in time when it is born or dies. Birth and death are to be interpreted as a change of state, which may develop over many years. In spite of the fact that languages are often compared to organisms which occur in nature, they are unlike living organisms as they are to a large extent constructed (and destroyed) by humans. Thus, languages emerge, develop, and disappear because of human involvement. Languages that existed 1,000 years ago have long ceased to exist, and today's living languages will not be around in another 1,000 years. Also, the languages of 100 years ago are not the same as today, and one may even notice differences between ten years ago and today. In any particular language, one can easily notice that the present generation is different from the previous one in their pronunciation and in the words they use. Yet this does not mean they speak a different language. In the long run, however, this is how a new language may emerge. While this may appear to be an entirely natural process, the human species plays a major role in steering it.

New languages appear on a daily basis, even though this goes largely unnoticed. New varieties are not immediately recognized as new languages, as they are preceded by a long process in which some varieties gain prestige and are being standardized. Successful varieties develop after a long struggle against another variety. Some varieties do not gain prestige and they are stigmatized as pidgins or creoles. A pidgin (probably from the Chinese pronunciation of 'business') is a simplified language which typically developed between groups that do not have a language in common. Most pidgins lack prestige and they serve a particular purpose only (usually trade). A pidgin differs from a creole, which is used as a first language and which has more purposes. A pidgin may develop into a creole through a process of nativization, when children acquire a pidgin as their native language. Yet there is no particular point in time which can be associated with the emergence of a creole as a separate language.[4] Trade languages can evolve into fully developed languages such as Lingala or Swahili, both of which are widely spoken in Eastern Africa and in parts of Congo.[5]

Afrikaans, as the language is known today, has also been described as a creole or as a partially creolized language.[6] Afrikaans evolved from the vernacular of South Holland spoken by Dutch settlers in what is now South Africa. In addition, it developed as a result of the interaction between European colonists, slaves imported from Africa and Asia, as well as indigenous Khoisan people. However, the contribution of the Khoikhoi (formerly known under the derogatory term *Hottentots*), slaves, and also the Muslim community in the development of Afrikaans has largely been neglected and even ignored.[7] Until the early twentieth century, Afrikaans was considered a Dutch dialect. Under South African law, Afrikaans was recognized as a distinct language, which replaced Standard Dutch as an official language in 1925. As observed earlier, the emergence of Afrikaans as a separate and standardized language is unique in the history of Western expansion. In addition, Afrikaans may be the only language that has a monument dedicated to it. The Afrikaans Language Monument (*Afrikaanse Taalmonument*), which was opened in 1975, commemorates the declaration of Afrikaans as an official language. Under the post-apartheid constitution, Afrikaans remains an official language, a status it has to share with English and nine other languages. In reality, the use of Afrikaans has been reduced in favour of English, which has become the de facto dominant language in South Africa.

The expansion of English all over the world has led to the emergence of many other varieties of English. First of all, English was exported to the New World by mother-tongue speakers of English from England, Wales, Scotland, and Ireland (the inner circle). Over time, the varieties spoken by these migrants were modified and they developed into today's American, Canadian, Australian, New Zealand, and South African Englishes. Although these are not different languages, they are clearly different varieties. These processes can also be observed in other colonial languages such as Spanish or Portuguese. The colonization of Asia and Africa led to the development of localized varieties of English (the outer circle), as happened in the Indian subcontinent. Some of these 'new Englishes' may be very difficult to understand for outsiders, including mother-tongue speakers of English. Many of the indigenized varieties of English are not standardized and they lack prestige. Eventually, however, they may mark the end of English as a unified language. They may develop into separate and official languages, as happened with Afrikaans. Something similar also happened with Latin, which gradually split into the Romance languages spoken today. Also, in the expanding circle, where the language is increasingly being used, English is adapted to local contexts. It may be too early to call these adaptations new varieties of English, as they are not standardized or officialised. Moreover, they lack prestige and they are generally considered 'bad English'. Yet voices have been raised to recognize some of these varieties as legitimized varieties of English. A good example could be Dutch

English, which – due to the widespread use of English in the Netherlands and the prestige of its speakers – could be accepted as a variety of English in its own right, as argued by Leiden-based linguist Alison Edwards.[8]

New varieties also emerge as particular groups establish their own identities, based on a common belief, social class, age, gender, or any other characteristic that marks them as being different from another group. Due to changing circumstances, new ways of communicating may emerge as well, both in speaking and in writing. Less than a generation ago, the internet did not exist, and the types of communication which virtually everyone is familiar with these days were unheard of. The very concept of a text message, for instance, would be very difficult to explain to a nineteenth-century writer, let alone the way vocabulary, grammar, and spelling are used in texting. Of course, this also works the other way round, as many of today's readers may find it difficult to read texts which were written by their parents or grandparents.

Language death

Technically speaking, a language dies when its last speaker dies. In most cases, however, language death is a protracted change of state. It may take decades or even centuries before a language becomes extinct, but it can be much faster as well. Although language death can be seen as a natural process, the pace at which languages are disappearing is unprecedented in human history. It has been predicted that up to 90 per cent of all languages in the world may have vanished by the end of this century.[9] *Ethnologue* lists 370 languages which have become extinct since 1950, which amounts to six languages a year. According to other sources, the situation is even more dramatic, and the loss could amount to one language every two weeks.[10] From an evolutionary perspective, this may be considered inevitable, as languages emerge, develop, and eventually disappear. On the other hand, concerns may be raised over the loss of biodiversity with regard to the coexistence of languages.[11] That is, the current pace at which languages disappear disturbs the ecological balance which is necessary to sustain a healthy system. Again, the human species has played a detrimental role in this process.

While the loss of a language may be perceived as a way of life, it can also be perceived as a tragedy. The latter view is expressed by Elias Canetti, the German-language author and Nobel Prize winner with a multilingual background. Born in Bulgaria to a Jewish family, they moved to England and afterwards to Austria, with interludes in Switzerland and Germany, and finally to England again to escape Nazi persecution. A native speaker of Ladino (also known as Judeo-Spanish), he spoke Bulgarian, English, and French, apart from German, his literary language. As Canetti observed:

> There is no such thing as an ugly language. Today I hear every language as if it were the only one, and when I hear of one that is dying, it overwhelms me as though it were the death of the Earth.[12]

Many other authors have expressed similar views, for instance the American writer James Crawford, according to whom 'the loss of a language represents the loss of a rare window on the human mind'.[13] While the latter view echoes ideas expressed by the German Romantics as well as Sapir and Whorf (see Chapters 2 and 3, respectively), it also reflects a genuine concern for the survival of endangered Native American and other languages. On the other hand, as argued by Steven Pinker, not all languages can be preserved, much in the same way as we cannot preserve every species on Earth, to which he adds 'we cannot preserve every language, and perhaps should not'.[14] Therefore, we might let the *linguistic universe do its stuff*.[15] Taken to the extreme, we could even argue that the only good language is a dead language. Or, as the Latin proverb reads, *lingua mortua sola lingua bona est*.

There is an obvious correlation between language death and globalization.[16] The cause of language death is often assimilation to a majority culture, which in today's world is the Anglo-American paradigm. Languages may survive more easily in areas not affected by globalization, such as the Amazon, where the highest concentration of Native American languages can be found. Yet language death is of all times and all places. It is slower in Africa and Asia than in Europe and its former settlement colonies. In Africa and Asia, fewer indigenous languages are threatened and they are typically endangered by other indigenous languages rather than by European colonial languages.[17] This may also explain why Papua New Guinea is the region with the highest number of languages in the world. While it has less than 8 million inhabitants, it has more than 800 languages. Apart from its geography (mountains, islands), political factors (weak central government) have also contributed to the region's rich linguistic diversity.[18]

Language death can have various causes. Languages may die of a 'natural cause' (e.g. when the last speaker dies), but they can also be 'killed', in which case the term 'homicide' may be more appropriate. People can give up their language voluntarily, which often happens when they migrate to another country. This may be a gradual process which can take two or even three generations. Whereas Greek emigrants in the United States kept their language over several generations, together with their culture and religion, Dutch emigrants assimilated very easily into the Protestant Anglo-Saxon culture. People can give up their language as a personal choice, conscious or unconscious, but they can also be forced to do so. For instance, slaves everywhere were the first to lose their ancestral languages. Sometimes their languages survive, or traces of the old language may live on in a newly developed language, as the example of Palenque showed (see Chapter 3). The languages of the powerless sometimes demonstrate more vitality than those of the powerful. This resilience may be due to the fact that these groups stick to their linguistic, cultural, or social identities.

In Europe, the emergence of the nation-state led to a reduction of the languages spoken by minorities. These languages lacked prestige, and they were suppressed as they did not fit in with the ideals of the emerging powers. This was the case in many countries, perhaps most notably in France, the United Kingdom, Spain, Italy, and Greece. Sometimes a language may become extinct in one country but survive in another country, as the example of Dutch shows. Whereas Dutch (or rather one of its Flemish variants) was wiped out in France in an effort to Frenchify the whole country, the language developed into one of the three standard languages of neighbouring Belgium, albeit after a long language struggle. The reason Dutch survived in Belgium (Flanders) but not in France is probably due to the fact that Dutch was the language of prestige in the Netherlands, whose standardized form was adopted in Belgium. Languages which have not been standardized and which are spoken in one region only have a much smaller chance of survival. This was the fate of most other minority languages in France, such as Breton and Corsican. Minority languages in the United Kingdom have not fared better. Manx and Cornish were declared extinct by the United Nations in 2009, and other languages, including Scottish Gaelic (not to be confused with Scots), are in dire straits as well.[19]

Similar tendencies can be observed all over the world. Yaghan (also known as Yámana) is one of the indigenous and near-extinct languages spoken in Tierra del Fuego, the archipelago off the southernmost tip of the South American mainland. Its name (which translates in English as 'Land of Fire') was given by Ferdinand Magellan, the Portuguese explorer and commander of the Spanish fleet, after seeing the Yaghans' fires along the shore. In the 1860s, more than 300 years after Magellan's arrival, British missionary and linguist Thomas Bridges set up a mission in Ushuaia. For 20 years, he lived among the Yaghans, where he compiled a Yaghan–English dictionary. These days, some 1,500 Yaghan descendants live around their ancestral grounds, but there is only one fluent speaker of Yaghan left. The last speaker is an 89-year-old woman who learned Spanish, the dominant and official language, when she was 9 years old. Her children were the first generation to grow up speaking Spanish, which in fact meant Spanish only. At that time, Yaghan speakers were mocked, as their language had no prestige at all. Recently, the government has encouraged the use and maintenance of Yaghan as well as other native languages. Yaghan is now taught in local kindergartens, but with only one fluent speaker left, the chances for survival may be slim.[20]

A language is endangered not only if there are fewer and fewer speakers, but also if the speakers do not identify with their language anymore or if the language is no longer used in a number of crucial domains (e.g. daily activities, celebrations). A language cannot survive if its speakers do not pass it on to their children. The story of Majid, a Syrian Kurd, may explain this in some more detail. The Kurds are the largest ethnic minority in Syria, comprising 7 to 10 per cent of the population. Majid grew up in northern Syria, bordering Turkey. Both of his parents were Kurds, but they had been 'Arabized' under the regime of Hafez al-Assad. As a result, he did not teach his children any Kurdish, and he even gave them Arab names. In addition, he and his family did not celebrate their traditional days anymore in order to get jobs with the Syrian authorities. The result was that they lost their Kurdish identity and language in just one generation.[21]

On the other hand, when speakers are motivated to pass on their language (and culture), an endangered language may become revitalized. So-called dead languages may live on in the culture and the literature they leave behind. This may be the case with languages such as Latin, ancient Greek, and Sanskrit. In the Renaissance, there was a revival of classical Latin and also Sanskrit had its revival. For other languages, there is even life after death, due to efforts to bring a language back to life in its spoken form. Sometimes a distinction is made between language revival and language revitalization. Whereas the former refers to the resurrection of a dead language (without any speakers), the latter refers to the rescue of a dying language. Hebrew may be the most successful example of language revival in the world. Although Hebrew had ceased to be an everyday spoken language by around AD 200, it survived into the medieval period as the language of Jewish liturgy and literature. In the nineteenth century, it was revived as a spoken and literary language and it became one of the two official languages of Israel (the other being Modern Standard Arabic). In today's Israel, Hebrew is the tool for upward mobility, whereas Arabic is a language of low prestige.[22]

In Europe, a more multilingual and multicultural policy has become standard in the last few decades, replacing the earlier practices of suppressing regional languages. Yet for many languages, it is too late. Languages such as Breton, Occitan, Basque, Sami, and Gaelic are still endangered, and one may get the impression they have been reanimated or kept alive artificially. One of the best known attempts at language revitalization in Europe concerns the Irish language. While earlier attempts to revitalize Irish were associated with Irish independence, contemporary attempts focus on education, where Irish is taught as a compulsory subject. Yet students do not acquire the fluency needed to turn Irish into a living language, and English is dominant through most of Ireland. Even though Manx and Cornish were declared extinct, efforts have been undertaken to revitalize these languages. Manx is now taught in primary and secondary schools, and cultural organizations have been created, such as the Manx Heritage Foundation (*Culture Vannin*). There have also been a number of attempts to revitalize the Cornish language. The irony is that the dominant power, whose aim was to wipe out these minority languages, is now involved in their rescue.

Another example of language revival is Basque (Euskara), a language spoken in Spain and France, on both sides of the western end of the Pyrenees. Euskara is very different from other languages in Europe as it does not have Indo-European roots. The language was revived after the Franco dictatorship in Spain. Franco wanted Euskara to disappear, and its speakers were humiliated, forced to pay fines, and taken to jail when they spoke the language. As a reaction, hidden Basque schools were set up (*ikastola*). Euskara has been used as a weapon, it has become politicized and manipulated by nationalists. The language was standardized in 1968, paving the way for writers to write in Euskara. In today's Spain, the language once prohibited by Franco is now printed in newspapers and spoken on the radio and television. Students in the region can choose whether to study in Euskara, Spanish, or both.

Language revitalization is not just a European phenomenon. In recent years, Native American tribes have been trying to revitalize their languages. At the other side of the world, the Māori in New Zealand have been doing the same with their language, *te reo Māori*. As a result of colonization, English was promoted as a means to speed up assimilation, and Māori was forbidden at schools until the 1970s, when a campaign was set up to teach the language in schools. Since the 1990s, a significant number of fluent speakers has emerged, making Māori more prominent in people's daily lives. Yet the dominance of English remains uncontested.

It should be noted that debates about language death and endangerment usually hide underlying political issues.[23] First, the concept of language death can be manipulated for nationalist purposes. In Slovenia, for instance, it is used to justify repressive monolingual policies and secure the local hegemony of Slovene, a small language (1.7 million L1 speakers) which is perceived as being threatened by other languages (e.g. by English in higher education). As a consequence, the survival of Slovene is equated to the survival of the nation.[24] Second, language revitalization policies can be a means to address the wrongs committed in the past towards linguistic minorities and aboriginals (such as the Inuit in Canada or the Māori in New Zealand). But they can also be a means to take control over natural or other resources. In fact, it may not be clear whose interests are being served. What is clear, however, is that discourses on language endangerment are often used as a political strategy, as part of an anti-colonialist struggle or resistance against the hegemony of a particular group or language. While an emerging nation-state – think of Catalonia – can promote its language for political reasons (to achieve more autonomy or independence), an existing nation-state – think of Spain in the Franco era – can suppress languages other than the national language as these languages can 'endanger' national unity.

Last but not least, it should be pointed out that the death of a language does not necessarily mean the death of a culture. People can still express their identities when their original language has disappeared, as evidenced by the vitality of black American culture in the United States. While it is impossible to try to preserve all languages in the world, as language death is natural and even inevitable, it is necessary to preserve the ecosystem between languages, as I will argue in Chapter 9.

Notes

1 Darwin (1859, 1987: 458).
2 Spencer (1864: 444).
3 Dil (1972).
4 Mufwene (2004).
5 Lingala is spoken in the Democratic Republic of the Congo (DRC, former Belgian colony) and in the Republic of Congo (former French colony); Swahili is spoken in the eastern part of the DRC.
6 Sebba (2007).
7 Painter (2010: 84–111).
8 Edwards (2016).
9 Mufwene (2004).
10 Dalby (2002).
11 Skutnabb-Kangas (2000).
12 Canetti (1987: 46).
13 Crawford (1995).

14 Pinker (1994: 258).
15 Barnes (2013: 100–101).
16 Mufwene (2004).
17 Mufwene (2004).
18 See:www.bbc.com/news/av/world-asia-46475671/which-country-has-the-most-languages (accessed 8 January 2019).
19 See: www.independent.co.uk/news/uk/this-britain/cornish-language-declared-extinct-by-un-1628244.html (accessed 18 February 2017) and www.unesco.org/languages-atlas/index.php# (accessed 18 February 2017).
20 See: www.bbc.com/travel/story/20180402-mamihlapinatapai-a-lost-languages-untranslatable-legacy. (accessed 6 January 2019).
21 Personal communication, Majid, 25 August 2018.
22 Or and Shohamy (2016).
23 Duchêne and Heller (2007).
24 Savski (2016).

9
TOWARDS AN ECOLOGICAL APPROACH TO LANGUAGE

Language and politics

Many ideas concerning language belong to the realm of myths. That is, they reflect people's beliefs about language rather than what language actually consists of. These beliefs are often embedded in other belief systems, which may be called ideologies. In this sense, Islam, Marxism, and free-market economics are all ideologies, as they seek to interpret (and possibly change) the world. Language is of crucial importance in any ideology, as it is a vehicle for conveying one's message to the world. The messages conveyed by Islam, Marxism, and free-market economics are radically different, and so is the language they use. For instance, when former Egyptian president Hosni Mubarak wanted to appeal to religious Muslims, he used Islamic metaphors and imagery in his language which wouldn't have worked in a Marxist or capitalist context. Likewise, the vocabulary, grammar, structure, and format (e.g. a sermon or a pamphlet) of a message are influenced by a particular ideology.

Although we speak of 'natural' languages, languages are not actually very natural at all. The ability to use language is often thought to be unique to the human species. Yet this may be a myth too. Basically, language is learned behaviour, and the way humans learn their mother tongues (literally the languages they learn from their mothers) is very similar to the way other animals learn their languages. Even birds learn to sing their songs by listening to and imitating the sounds made by their parents. If a sound doesn't come out right the first time, the parents provide feedback and the bird whistles it higher or lower next time. This is also how humans learn to talk. It remains a matter of debate whether the communication of birds and other species may be called language. Apart from the obvious physical and cognitive differences between the species, all of them have developed highly effective means of communication. The main difference between animal talk and human talk appears to be that humans can use language in a less utilitarian and more abstract way. Bertrand Russell, the English philosopher and mathematician, put it as follows: 'No matter how eloquently a dog may bark, he cannot tell you that his parents were poor but honest'.[1] Yet animal talk may not be as primitive as we humans assume. After all, we can only judge animal talk from our own perspective. As the most powerful animal in the world, we often regard our perspective as the only one which counts. But this may be a naïve belief in our own superiority, and some modesty is probably needed. If we want to understand animals, we might as well learn their languages instead of trying to teach them ours – an endeavour which is bound to fail anyway, as the example of Nim Chimpsky revealed.

Unlike other animals, humans use language to construct their own narratives (or *stories*, to use a more popular term). Humans do this to make sense of their world. In all great ideologies, language plays a quintessential role in making up these stories. These ideologies – which might be based on religion or on political or economic systems – are also used to develop group identities. Ideologies are mutually exclusive belief systems: one cannot, for instance, be a Christian and a Muslim at the same time. Likewise, Marxism and neo-liberalism are incompatible. The narratives clash, as all of them claim to be the one and only truth. In spite of their potentially devastating effects, we need those stories. Without narratives, we would have no literature, and no art or culture either. However, stories should serve us, and not the other way round. Problems arise when humans take the stories they have created themselves to be the infallible words of a prophet or guru. Throughout history, millions of people have been butchered in the name of God, or of Allah, or some other competing ideologies.

We need language in order to be able to assign meaning to narratives. Without it, stories – and thus ideologies – cannot be imagined. Philosophies, religions, and political, social, and economic systems need language to express their ideas. Otherwise they would be powerless, and they could not attract the masses of followers they need. Language is at the core of world literature, and of political, religious, and other texts which seek to explore the meaning of life. Moreover, without language it is impossible to imagine ourselves and to construct identities. We use it to construct basic relationships in which the in-groups ('we') and the out-groups ('they') are clearly defined. We use names to refer to ourselves and other people, where they come from, what language they speak, and so on. In many languages, one's own language is referred to simply as *language*, as though there were no others. In Quechua, for instance, the very word *Quechua* means 'human speech'.[2] Last but not least, we have the myth of language as a rigid or monolithic structure.[3] While this has proved to be a useful fiction for language managers (both linguists and language advisory bodies such as the French Academy), it remains a false belief. One of the essential characteristics of language is *change*. And what's more, languages are *made* by their users, as are the differences between languages. Names are given to languages to distinguish them from one another, and their differences are laid down in dictionaries, grammars, and pronunciation guides. This process of institutionalizing differences is commonly called standardization.

I'd like to come back to the written form of a language: its script or the alphabet used. This is the most visible sign of a language and can often be recognized immediately, even by those who cannot read or speak the language at all. Whereas Latin and its alphabet were once seen as the language of the Western world and its culture (in which Christianity featured prominently), this is no longer the case. The West has largely become a secular world, and the Latin alphabet is no longer associated with religion. As a matter of fact, the Latin alphabet is now used all over the world for pragmatic and often commercial purposes – just think of the dominance of English as the language of international business. Many languages have their own scripts, which are often used for cultural or religious purposes and which serve as strong markers of their identity. This is the case, for instance, for Chinese characters and the Arabic script, both of which have developed strong traditions of calligraphy, a tradition which has almost been lost in today's Western world. Thus, a language or its script can be the carrier of a whole culture. Arabic, for instance, is the language of Islam, even in non-Arabic-speaking countries such as Turkey, where Arabic and its script have a prominent place in mosques, monuments, and so on (even though very few can read or understand it).

There has been a long evolution from the 'primitive' forms of communication used by our ancestors millions of years ago to the standardized languages we know today. It should be repeated here that the notion of a standard language is essentially a European concept, which has its roots in the centuries when Europe dominated the world (roughly from the sixteenth century onwards) and which came into full flower in the nineteenth century, the era of nation-building. Lexicographers, grammarians, and spelling and style gurus of all kinds determined what made for correct language and what did not. These highly ideological practices served the interests of state- and nation-builders, as language is after all an effective means of imagining one's community. Today's *superdiverse* world is very different from their world, which was dominated by elderly, white, male, Christian, upper- and middle-class speakers of Western languages, especially Spanish, Portuguese, French, and English.

As observed by Pierre Bourdieu, language is a mechanism of power. The pecking order of today's languages in the world shows that they are not equal, and that there are frictions between languages, language groups, and the civilizations they are embedded in. In the 'clash of civilizations', according to the hypothesis put forward by Samuel Huntington, the world's major conflicts occur between different religions, economic systems, and languages.[4] The most widely used languages originated in Europe and spread all over the globe as a result of colonialism. On the other continents, there are far more languages than in Europe, but they tend to be less standardized. Many of these languages are likely to become extinct in the foreseeable future due to the dominance of other languages which have more speakers, prestige, and power.

In today's world, English has become the *hypercentral* language. There is not a single language that has more speakers (though most use English as a second language), prestige, or power. As the language of globalization, English means access to the world. The use of English is often informed by pragmatic or commercial interests, even in education. Yet the commodification of education ('English sells') does not necessarily imply better learning or teaching, or better communication.

English is sometimes seen as the killer language (or the Tyrannosaurus rex, the ultimate predator), but the language does provide new opportunities for users as well. As a lingua franca, English may be regarded as everyone's language, and not just the language of its 'native' speakers (I use inverted commas to indicate that the use of this word is problematic, as I discussed earlier). In other words, English is the language everyone can use when communicating with people they do not have another language in common with. In such a setting, the rules are no longer set by 'native' speakers, but by the communities of practice themselves. Unfortunately, not all speakers are equally fluent in English, and some varieties may have more prestige than other varieties. Chinese English, for instance, carries more stigma than some varieties of English spoken in Europe (e.g. Scandinavian English, which carries very little stigma). As a result, new inequalities may be created. Apparently, English is not the equalizer it is often believed to be, and it is not even a real lingua franca (i.e. a language that *all* people have in common).

Instead of taking it for granted that everyone speaks English, more language sensitivity is needed. We should learn other people's languages to understand not only what they say, but also their culture. For instance, no one can imagine a foreign correspondent based in the United States who cannot speak English. This is simply impossible. Yet this is exactly what happens in other parts of the world. Most foreign correspondents in the Middle East or in China are presented as specialists in the region but do not speak Arabic or Chinese at all. The few of them who do have access to these languages also understand the cultures and their underlying subtleties far better than other correspondents, who have to rely on translators. In a recent British movie set in the Stalin era, everyone in the Kremlin speaks English, including Stalin himself.[5] Could you imagine a movie set in the White House in which everyone speaks Russian?

In today's world, there are more language- and culture-related conflicts than ever before. This is due to globalization, as a result of which civilizations clash and compete for dominance. Whereas in the past some European countries exported their religions, cultures, and languages to all other parts of the world, European values are no longer regarded as universal. Moreover, the way that European countries imposed their languages and cultures on their colonies can hardly be seen as exemplary. The use of brute force can work in the short term, but it doesn't last. There is some irony in the fact that France's efforts to Frenchify the rest of Europe and many other parts of the world resulted in the demise of French as a global language, something many French people find difficult to accept. The times, however, are changing. President Macron is the first French head of state to have addressed his audience in English on several of his foreign visits, including to Germany and the United States. Even though the president was heavily criticized for speaking English by his right-wing opponents in France, his sense of realism was interpreted as statesmanship in the rest of the world.

Efforts to protect a language are often made in vain and can even be counterproductive, as the French example shows. Throughout history, thousands of languages have emerged and disappeared. Although from a Darwinian perspective this may be called a natural process, the pace at which languages and cultures are disappearing has never been so high in history and may be truly alarming. However, merely protecting a language does not work if its speakers are not convinced of the value of their language. Speaking only one language does not suffice either. Contrary to popular opinion, most people are multilingual. Different languages or varieties of the same language are used in different contexts with different speakers. The more languages one speaks, the more worlds one has access to.

Language and ecology

Ernst Haeckel, a nineteenth-century German biologist, has been credited with having invented the word 'ecology'.[6] The word, which derives from Greek οἶκος (house or environment) and λογία (study of), was rendered in German as Öcologie by Haeckel in 1866 and imported into English as *ecology* about a decade later. Another German scholar, Alexander von Humboldt, the famous explorer and Haeckel's contemporary, is often considered the father of ecology (mysteriously, but like most other inventions, ecology does not appear to have a mother). In his approach to nature, Humboldt stressed the interconnectedness of things. Unlike earlier approaches, he took into account the wider context, including the natural environment, the people living in it, and their culture. This involves not only the surface level (what can be seen), but also what lies beneath, where invisible changes can have huge effects. His brother, the linguist Wilhelm von Humboldt, took a similar approach to language, though this was unfortunately discredited by later nationalist narratives (see Chapter 3).

An ecological approach to language sees humans as part of the larger ecosystems that life depends on. In much the same way that humans should exist in harmony with their natural environment, humans and their languages should exist in harmony too. The concept of ecological linguistics was introduced in the 1970s by Einar Haugen, an American linguist of Norwegian descent. Haugen defined language ecology studies as the 'interactions between any given language and its environment'.[7] Key ecological questions deal with a language's classification (i.e. its relation to other languages), its users (e.g. class, gender), its domains of use (e.g. politics, religion), the other languages employed concurrently by its users, the internal varieties of a language (some of which may have more prestige than others), the nature of its written traditions (some languages have a long written tradition, others are oral only), the degree to which its written form has been standardized, the institutional support it has won (from governments and educational institutions, but also through private language management), the attitudes towards the language (e.g. regarding its status), and the typology of ecological classification.

Perhaps the most crucial concept in the ecological language approach is language diversity. As in nature, diversity is crucial to the survival of a species, and monoculture can lead to disaster, poor health, and death. Due to the forces of globalization, dominant languages have spread and replaced local languages more quickly than ever before. The most striking example of this linguistic imperialism is, of course, English, the language which has outdone all others. While English may sometimes be spread actively and deliberately, it is also a 'natural' phenomenon in that English means prestige, power, and access to the world. That also explains why this book was written in English. But in order to protect linguistic and cultural diversity, it is important to foster local languages as well. The term 'local' is relative, as some of these languages are used by millions of people. Other languages may have only a couple of speakers left, and these languages are certainly doomed. One of the goals of ecolinguistic research is to protect both cultural diversity and the linguistic diversity that supports it.[8]

The United Nations proclaimed 2019 as the International Year of Indigenous Languages in order to raise awareness of them, and because they make an important contribution to the world's rich cultural and linguistic diversity. However, many of these languages are in danger of disappearing as indigenous people are often isolated, both linguistically and politically, but also socially, geographically, historically, and culturally. Yet they represent complex systems of knowledge and communication, which could and should be recognized as important recourses for development, peace-building, and reconciliation. In addition, many indigenous peoples play a crucial role in protecting the world's unique ecosystems.[9] (Unfortunately, sometimes they use their natural resources in unsustainable ways, which somehow contradicts the idea of indigenous people as natural conservationists.)

An ecological language approach ties in with the concept of posthumanism. Contrary to what this term appears to suggest, posthumanism does not give up on humanity, but it aims to rethink the relationship between humans and other animals, humans and nature, and also humans and artefacts (such as prosthetic limbs). As Alastair Pennycook argues, these divisions are neither helpful nor sustainable in today's world.[10] The traditional notion of humanism, which originated in fourteenth-century Europe, reflects a Western anthropocentric view that is untenable in a world in which the centre of power is shifting away from the West. Therefore, the West can no longer assume the universality of its values.[11] Moreover, being human has all too often been reduced to hu*man*, as the world was – and is – dominated by men. Or, more specifically, by white men from WEIRD countries (Western, educated, industrialized, rich, and democratic). What we need is a more humble and inclusive sense of humanism.

First and foremost, we should rethink our relation with other animals and the world we share with them. The Chomskyan assumption that language is what separates humans from animals does not hold. In spite of the distinctive qualities of human language, there is no sharp divide between human and animal communication.[12] Yet this division is firmly rooted in Western culture, which focuses on the 'intellectual' senses based on sight and sound, and not on the more 'bodily' senses (smell, taste, touch) which have traditionally been associated with animals, other races, and women.[13] This distinction is reflected in language, which puts emphasis on writing and reading skills (based on sight) and listening and speaking (based on sound), while other ways of communication are completely neglected and considered inferior. This explains the struggle of the Deaf, whose languages were discriminated against because they were not considered 'real' languages as they lack the sound component.

The current linguistic ecosystem is clearly out of balance. While it may be impossible to create a system in which all languages and their users are equal, it is feasible to restore the balance. For instance, while English may be the best and even only option when no other lingua franca is available, there are cases when another language might be more appropriate. This is clear in contexts where English has been imposed due to its perceived prestige or advantages, but where it has no real added value. It could even be counterproductive, for example when two people are forced to use English when communicating with each other at work despite being speakers of the same language (i.e. any language other than English). The example may sound far-fetched, but it is in fact surprisingly common.

An ecological approach to language should also pay attention to power relations between languages and between the users of these languages. The balance should be restored, and people should have equal linguistic opportunities. Education can play a crucial role in achieving this objective. Moreover, students should be taught to be critical of the world they live in. Priority should be given to the victims of unequal power relations, and the perpetrators should be unmasked. While this may not prevent another Hitler or Milošević from seizing power, it is important to reveal such tyrants' abuse of power and language.

Education is of seminal importance. It is far more than what happens in a classroom; perhaps most learning – especially informal learning – takes place outside of a classroom, in fact. In today's world, learning entails growing up to become a citizen of the world we live in, a world which is increasingly multicultural and multilingual. Exposure to other cultures and languages and the willingness to participate in this process are therefore of the utmost importance. Unfortunately, many people or groups of people lock themselves up in their own cultures and languages. We see this in today's most affluent societies, most of which are not very welcoming towards 'newcomers' such as refugees or asylum seekers. Many of these people don't manage to make a decent living because of socio-economic and other reasons, but also because of their cultural and linguistic backgrounds. The ensuing clash of civilizations leads to a *tribalization* of society that is characterized by the rejection of otherness, which leads to more segregation instead of integration. One of the main tasks of education in the era of globalization is to teach mutual tolerance and respect for the other. This may sound utopian, but failure to do so will result in even more division.

An ecological approach to language does not advocate some kind of naïve return to nature. On the contrary, it is based in the real world, a world it aims to save for future generations. It is also an approach which recognizes diversity as one of its key assets. We should abandon the centrifugal idea that we are the centre around which the world revolves. This holds for the human species in general as well as for entities created by humans, such as nations. Great nations typically regard themselves as the centre of the world, as can be observed in how they map the world. Maps produced in Europe from the sixteenth century onwards place Europe at the centre of the world, whereas on Chinese maps it is China that is in the middle. Even the name the Chinese have given to their country reflects this view: 中国 (Zhongguo, 'China'), which literally means 'middle country'. Note that in the Chinese character for middle (中, zhong), the square is neatly divided through the middle too.

We should move away from the centre, *our* centre. In an ecological approach, we are not alone in the centre – perhaps we are not in the centre at all. The belief that one is in the centre (or deserves to be) has led to local conflicts and even full-scale wars. Personal ambitions do not leave much space for other people's aspirations. Contemporary nation-states, which are the basis of today's world organizations, emerged from external and internal power conflicts in the past, and some of these conflicts are still smouldering. Even today, many of these nation-states show disrespect for their linguistic and regional minorities, who often face persecution. This is even the case in highly civilized countries such as Spain, a country which nevertheless has a long history of intolerance towards its minorities, and is currently preventing Catalonia from seeking independence.

Emotions tend to run high over conflicts involving language and identity, and it may be difficult to reach a compromise. Decisions are usually enforced by the most powerful party. Yet language users may benefit from an ecological attitude towards language, and decisions should never be informed purely by political, economic, or commercial interests. Language use should be governed by what is feasible or appropriate in a given context, and some compromise may be necessary. In some contexts, the use of English may be preferred, but this will not necessarily be the case in another context. It may also depend on the *domain*, with its particular needs or formats. For instance, business, politics, and academia have very different needs regarding the use of a particular language or language variety. When publishing an article in a journal, 'correct' language will be a prerequisite, whereas in a discussion or debate the most important issue will be to get one's message across. Last but not least, it all depends on the people involved: the language users. As language managers, they have to cope with all the subtleties involved in communication, including power relations and hidden ideologies. Again, education is of seminal importance: people should be taught not only to use language in an appropriate way, but also to understand the subtleties underlying communication. The issue at stake is that communication takes place in contexts which are never neutral and always culturally and politically embedded.

In today's globalizing world, new means of communicating with people who speak different languages are necessary. It is often thought that English will do the job or a new variety of English, serving as everyone's lingua franca. Yet this is what Pennycook refers to as the myth of English as the international language of communication. As he points out, English can also be understood as the language of global miscommunication.[14] This also holds for new varieties of English. It is highly unlikely that English as a lingua franca (often abbreviated as ELF, and sometimes nicknamed as *Elfish*) will be able to serve as everyone's language, and new inequalities are bound to emerge. After all, some varieties of English (even non-'native' ones) have more prestige than others. To paraphrase Orwell, one might say that all Englishes are equal, but some are more equal than others.

As an alternative to speaking English or Elfish, it has been suggested that people speak the language they know best and which their interlocutor understands but may not be able to speak fluently. For instance, Scandinavians could communicate in their own languages instead of in English. The same could work between other related languages, such as German and Dutch. In practice, however, people may still prefer to use English, as this is what they have become accustomed to. In addition, speaking English may have more prestige. Another option is *parallel lingualism*, which is the parallel use of several languages, depending on the context. The term was coined around the turn of the century in the Nordic countries, where the policy was also adopted for the first time.[15] Parallel language use is often applied in higher education, where the national language can be used in parallel with another language, usually English. Although the policy has been recommended at both national and supranational levels, some argue that parallel language is a political slogan rather than an effective language policy.[16]

Language is a tremendous force, one which can be used to manipulate people and even entire communities. Preachers of all kinds can turn the faithful into crusaders or terrorists, and political agitators can turn entire societies into dystopias. What these ideologies have in common is that they are based on exclusiveness (us versus them). One's own system is held up as the best (e.g. the 'free world'), while the other is dehumanized (e.g. they become 'infidels' or 'crimmigrants', a combination of *criminal* and *immigrant*). But language can also be used to shape dreams and paint a picture of a better world based on inclusiveness. In such a world, language can be a liberating force.

Notes

1 At least, Russell is claimed to have said this, but I couldn't find the original source. The quotation can be found in, for instance, Evans (2016: 23).
2 Ostler (2006: 356).
3 Haugen (1972).
4 Huntington (1996).
5 *The Death of Stalin* (2017). See: www.youtube.com/watch?v=ukJ5dMYx2no (accessed 11 November 2018). It should be added that the use of English in *The Death of Stalin* is done with tongue in cheek, as everyone speaks in over-the-top accents – Stalin in a cockney accent, Zhukov in a broad northern English accent, and Khrushchev in a New York accent.
6 Wulf (2015: 307).
7 Haugen (1972).
8 See: www.terralinguaubuntu.org (accessed 10 January 2019).
9 See: https://en.iyil2019.org (accessed 8 March 2019).
10 Pennycook (2018: 14).

11 Chakrabarty (2000) argues in favour of the *provincialization* of Europe: we have to put Europe (and the West in general) in its rightful place in the world, which is no longer at the centre.
12 Evans (2016: 429).
13 Classen et al. (1994).
14 Pennycook (2018: 90).
15 Hultgren et al. (2014).
16 Kuteeva (2014).

PART 2
Personal language histories

1 Aim and scope

The focus in this part is on 11 individual language users from all over the world, with an emphasis on speakers from developing countries. The speakers represent a myriad of languages and language practices. Their stories – or personal language histories, as I have labelled them – illustrate several of the issues dealt with in Part 1. However, they are more than mere illustrations: the stories reveal individual perceptions and biases towards languages and language varieties as well as towards their speakers. The stories show that most speakers are proud of their linguistic and cultural identity and that they feel strongly about their 'own' language or dialect. In addition, they appear to have multiple linguistic identities, as individuals can have different identities in different languages, and even within one language identities are layered. Linguistic identities do not stand apart, but they are interconnected with other identities such as ethnicity, social class, and gender.

The countries discussed in this part are highly multilingual, and so are the individual speakers (most of them speak at least three languages). In many of these countries, languages which originated in Europe – and which played a major role in the colonization of the world – still play a prominent role as a lingua franca or as a language of the ruling elite. All speakers speak at least one of the languages listed in the top five most powerful languages worldwide: English, Chinese, French, Spanish, and Arabic (see Chapter 5). In all narratives, English plays a crucially important role. Even though very few (if any) of the speakers speak English as their first language, they can all communicate in English. All in all, the speakers represent more than 20 different languages, including some smaller and lesser-known languages.

The personal language histories reflect interviews which were conducted orally (face to face), written (by email), or a combination of both. The interviewees were encouraged to reflect on their own language practices. The focus is on the interviewees' linguistic repertoire – that is, all languages and language varieties she or he speaks. The interviews deal with the context in which a particular language is used (e.g. school and work), the prestige of a language, its role as an identity marker, and the role of English in the interviewees' lives. In the language histories, I tried to make audible the *voice* of the interviewees, in that the replies reflect the words they used as well as their tone. As each interview has its own dynamics – and can be considered as being jointly constructed by the interviewee and the interviewer – the interviews take different forms.

English appears to be increasingly important for all of the interviewees, as it is generally considered to be the language of globalization and access to the world. It is often the language of (higher) education as well, and speaking English often adds to the speakers' prestige (particularly in Asia and Africa). The speakers' command of English tends to vary considerably. Even among those who were educated in English, there are huge differences in English language proficiency, due do the education system and other factors. It should be added that the interviewees may be called privileged because of their knowledge of English, which provides access to education and, ultimately, to the world. This also explains why the voices of those who are less educated and who have less or no access to English are absent in these narratives.

The interviews are with speakers from all continents, representing not only different languages, but also different cultures, religions, and political and economic systems. The focus, however, is on individual speakers and on the languages they use. Even though the speakers represent a particular group or speech community, they should be seen as individuals with specific language practices. The first three interviews are with speakers from the Asian continent (the Philippines, Taiwan, India), then there are three with speakers from the African continent (Egypt, Tanzania, Burundi), one from the Pacific (New Zealand), two from Latin America (Nicaragua, Cuba), and two from Europe (Kosovo, Denmark). The selection of interviewees aims to represent the diversity of language practices all over the world, but of course many other examples could have been provided. As stated in the introductory chapter, readers are welcome to submit their own language histories so that a fuller picture of language practices worldwide can be provided.

The purpose of this part is to let the interviews speak for themselves, and therefore no further commentary has been provided (apart from short introductory paragraphs). In order to protect the interviewees' privacy, their names have been changed and/or only the first letter of their family name has been given, unless they agreed to use their full names.

More information about the personal language histories can be found here: www.routledge.com/9780367365424

2 Asia

Ifugao, the Philippines

> *The Ifugaos are here to stay!*
>
> (Dulnuan A.)

Under Spanish colonial rule, which lasted for more than three centuries, Spanish was the official language of the Philippines. Following the American occupation and the imposition of English, the use of Spanish gradually declined, especially after the 1940s. In 1987, Filipino was declared the national language. It is based on Tagalog, the most widely spoken language, but it incorporates Western influences such as Spanish and English words. Moreover, languages are often mixed. As a Filipino from Metro Manila (the capital area) told me, 'If someone asks me how many grapes I'd have for a snack, I answer in Filipino or in English if it is between 1 and 10 pesos. If it is 11 to 20 pesos, I'll answer in Spanish. But usually, if the number is higher, something greater than 50, I'll answer in English'. Filipino as well as English are official languages, but English is seen as a status symbol. As my interviewee conceded, 'You look more professional, educated and even smart if you speak English well'. Apart from the languages mentioned here, dozens of other languages and dialects are spoken all over the country.

The Ifugaos, a people known for their rich oral literary traditions, live in the south-eastern part of the Cordillera region in the north of the Philippines. The region is well known for its rice terraces, one of the country's major tourist attractions. Ifugao is often described as a dialect continuum (meaning that one variety slowly changes into another variety), even though its main varieties are sometimes considered separate languages. One of these varieties is Tuwali, which is spoken by some 30,000 Ifugaos.

I talked to Dulnuan A., an environmental planner from Ifugao and a native speaker of Tuwali. As a member of an indigenous tribe, he has been exposed to social injustice and inequality. Outside their province, the Ifugaos are often mocked because most of them are not Tagalog speakers. Yet they take great pride in their local languages and their culture. As Dulnuan explains, Ifugao derives from *ipugo*, which literally means 'from the hill', which one can easily understand considering the landscape. Yet it can also mean 'people from the earth' (i.e. mortals or humans) as distinguished from the other worlds the Ifugaos believed in, such as the 'skyworld', the world of the spirits and deities.

In spite of its relatively small number of speakers, Tuwali is a vigorous language which is spoken in all domains: 'We speak it everywhere, at home, at school, at work, at social functions, even in church'. Even though *Ethnologue* lists Tuwali as a language,[1] Dulnuan perceives it as a dialect 'because it is only us as a particular ethnolinguistic group that speaks it'. Nevertheless, his attitude towards his language and culture is very positive. First and foremost, he associates Ifugao with ingenuity, as the Ifugaos have built 'a world heritage without slave labour that has been sustained for more than 2,000 years'. The other keyword Dulnuan mentions is resilience. He notes that 'many indigenous peoples around the world have been driven out of their places or they have even become extinct. But the Ifugaos are here to stay!'

In the Ifugao region, Tuwali is often used as a lingua franca, as the speakers of related languages such as Ayangan or Kalanguya can usually speak Tuwali, whereas speakers of Tuwali usually do not speak the other languages. As Dulnuan explains, this may be due to the fact that most of the urban centres are located in the Tuwali areas. This is where government offices and educational and other important institutions are based as well. As a result, speakers of the other languages are more exposed to Tuwali than the other way round. Moreover, Dulnuan thinks Tuwali is easier to learn.

Apart from Tuwali, Dulnuan speaks Tagalog, Ilocano (a language spoken by most people in the northern Philippines), and English, which he speaks and writes fluently. Whereas English is used in an official capacity as well as in everyday conversations, Tagalog and Ilocano are used in everyday conversations but never in written official use. Dulnuan associates English with globalization, Tagalog with optimism, and Ilocano with togetherness.

Thane, India

> *English is related to social class.*
>
> (Sonya Ochaney)

Maharashtra is the wealthiest and the most industrialized state of India. Its capital, the sprawling metropolis of Mumbai (formerly known as Bombay), is the seat of the Bollywood film industry. The state's official language is Marathi, which varies locally (Marathi has more than 40 dialects, many of which share features with other languages).[2] Moreover, different regions have their own language. While the number of Marathi-speakers has declined in recent years, the number of Hindi-speakers has risen. In urban areas, English is widely used.

Sonya Ochaney comes from Thane, a metropolitan city and the immediate neighbour of Mumbai, where she studied sociology. She speaks English, Hindi, and Marathi, as well as some Sindhi, which she describes as her mother tongue.

> *Which language do you consider to be your main language?*

> I would consider Hindi and English to be my main languages. Most of the conversations I have are in those two languages. These two languages were spoken at home, school, college, and my workplace. I have learnt Marathi in school and can speak it well. But within my sphere of work, family, and social circle, I speak Hindi and English more. This is also because Thane and Mumbai are cosmopolitan in nature, hence Marathi isn't spoken by everyone. Marathi is the official language, but in daily usage it isn't used so much. If I visited a government office, I would have to speak in Marathi (if I wanted my work done faster, for instance). Otherwise there are many migrants living in

these two areas and Hindi and English are understood more. English is related to social class, Hindi isn't.

How well do you speak Sindhi?

I can understand Sindhi and speak it in broken sentences, but I cannot read or write it. It is a language spoken by a small population in India (it is a minority language). This is because many of them migrated to India during the partition. Sindhi is still spoken in certain pockets of Pakistan as well. My parents studied in Sindhi-medium schools.

How would you rate English in terms of prestige?

English is considered prestigious amongst the others I mentioned. But that would probably be in the cities or major towns in India. It is considered important for jobs in multinational companies and such other organizations, but locally I'm not so sure of it. Also, English is taught in private schools (which are more expensive) as compared to the government-aided schools which largely emphasize local languages. Hence it is connected to social classes/status since not all families can afford a private school.

How come your English is so good?

I went to a private school. We were given English lessons with an emphasis on grammar and sentence constructions. This is one major reason. Another reason is the fact that I enjoyed reading. I would spend my days reading different novels and that is where I picked up most of my English. I also had people around me to speak it with and this helped me improve. For many Indians, their schools focus on vernacular languages and English is taught at a later stage. Also, they may be reading books in those languages and may not have anyone in the family to practise English with.

Can you, as a speaker of Hindi, communicate with people from Pakistan who speak Urdu?

Yes, I can communicate with people from Pakistan. They understand Hindi as well and we can understand a little bit of Urdu.

Do you consider Hindi and Urdu to be the same language?

Hindi and Urdu are not the same language, I think. There are many Urdu words that Hindi has co-opted, but I'm not sure if they are completely the same. Urdu is used more for poetry and in many Bollywood songs because it sounds better, but I don't know anyone around me who can speak fluent Urdu.

Do you sometimes mix languages?

There are many times we use something now called Hinglish (i.e. a mixture of Hindi and English). We either swap between the two languages or use English words while talking Hindi, and vice versa. Informally it is done all the time without even batting an eyelid. An example of Hinglish would be 'Chal na ("come on") let's go'. It is common to end sentences with *na* (Hindi word): 'Tell me something na'. Of course, this is an informal way of communicating.

Taipei, Taiwan

Twinkle, Twinkle, Little Star

Formerly known as *Ilha Formosa* ('beautiful island' in Portuguese), Taiwan has seen its fair share of foreign occupiers. The island, which was inhabited by aborigines of Malayan descent, was opened by the Spaniards and the Dutch to mass Han immigration from the Chinese mainland in the seventeenth century. After a brief spell as a Dutch colony, the island was administered by China's Qing dynasty (1683–1895). As a result of the Sino-Japanese War (1895), the island was ceded to Japan. Following the Japanese surrender after the Second World War, the Republic of China took control. When the Republic lost mainland China to the communists in 1949, the nationalists fled to Taiwan and continued their claim to be the legitimate government of China. Communist China, on the other hand, claimed (and still claims) its sovereignty over Taiwan as part of its One China policy.[3] Until 1971, Taiwan (also known as the Republic of China, or the ROC) represented China at the UN, when it lost its seat to the People's Republic of China (PRC). While the PRC denies the existence of Taiwan as an independent country, Taiwan boasts a strong sense of independence.

Apart from their Chinese name, many ethnically Chinese people adopt an English first name as well, which is mainly used to communicate with foreigners. My interviewee's present English name, Sherry, was chosen by her teacher in kindergarten. Previously, she had another English name, which had been chosen by her mother, but the teacher changed that name because it sounded 'weird' (she does not remember the other name, though). Many of her Chinese friends use her present English name as well. As Sherry states, 'it doesn't make any difference what name they call me'.

Like many people in Taiwan (especially young people), Sherry considers herself to be Taiwanese rather than Chinese. This is also how she introduces herself to foreigners. Even though Sherry claims she is not interested in politics, this very idea of two distinct identities could be interpreted as an outspoken political view which lends credibility to the idea of an independent Taiwan. As far as her spoken language is concerned, she prefers a Taiwanese accent to the standard accent of mainland China. The latter is often considered to be more 'aggressive', while a Taiwanese accent is considered 'gentler'. Sherry is a speaker of Mandarin (the official language of Taiwan), but she can speak some Taiwanese as well.

Sherry lives in Taipei, the capital of Taiwan, in a middle-class family. Currently, Sherry is a first-year student of food science, but later she plans to continue her education in the United States. Many of her friends actually study in the United States, after having invested heavily in learning English first. Like in mainland China and many other Asian countries, English language learning is a booming market in Taiwan, and huge amounts of money are spent on English language training and examination preparation. Sherry's parents, who do not speak English at all, have invested in English language education for their children from a very young age.

Kindergarten was the place where Sherry picked up her first English words. One of the first songs she remembers from kindergarten is 'Twinkle, Twinkle, Little Star', a popular English lullaby which is well known in Taiwan as well, where it is often used for teaching purposes. Other popular songs include 'London Bridge is Falling Down' and 'Yankee Doodle', two songs which are not particularly related to Asian culture. The bookshelves in her parents' home are lined with fairy tales and DVDs in English, which are now being used by her younger sister. In fact, they have more books in English than in Chinese. When she was 14, her parents sent her to Greenwich in the United Kingdom to attend a language course. Although Sherry thought the trip was great fun, she admits she didn't learn too much English as she mainly communicated in Chinese with her Taiwanese classmates.

Like many of her friends, Sherry often uses English words when speaking Chinese. For instance, instead of using the Chinese words for 'water' or 'beautiful' she uses them in English, at least in an informal setting:

> 可以給我 water 嗎? (Pinyin:[4] ke yi gei wo [water] ma; English: May I have a glass of water?) Wow, 你今天好beautiful. (Pinyin: [wow] ni jin tian hao [beautiful]; English: You look so beautiful today.)

Other English words which are often used in a Chinese sentence include 'challenge', 'highlight', 'topic', and even 'maybe'. Even though these words do not add anything from a communicative point of view, they are used to sound professional, cool, or hip.

3 Africa

Cairo, Egypt

It makes me happy when I can speak Arabic.

(Ruth Vandewalle)

With over 97 million inhabitants, Egypt is the most populous country in North Africa and in the Arab world. It is a predominantly Muslim country with a significant Christian minority. The official language is Arabic. From the sixteenth to the beginning of the twentieth century, Egypt was ruled by the Ottoman Empire and the British Empire, respectively. Following the 1952 revolution, Egypt was declared a republic. Throughout the second half of the twentieth century, the country was plagued with political, social, and religious turmoil. The 2011 revolution led to the overthrow of President Hosni Mubarak, who had ruled the country with an iron fist for almost 30 years. After an initial period of hope for democratic change, increased instability in the aftermath of the revolution eventually led to the current authoritarian regime of President Abdel Fattah el-Sisi.

A fluent speaker of Arabic, Belgian-born Ruth Vandewalle works in Egypt as a documentary producer for Dutch television. In addition, she is a correspondent for Flemish television and occasionally she works for CNN. Apart from Arabic, Dutch (her native language), and English, which she is fluent in, she can get by in French. Based in Cairo, where she has been living for ten years, Ruth travels widely in Egypt and in the Arabic-speaking world.

Ruth insists on speaking Arabic with other speakers of Arabic, even if they speak English, as this is the only way to fully master a language. Speaking English is just too easy. 'It makes me happy when I can speak Arabic', Ruth concedes. And she continues, 'Arabic is a very expressive and poetic language. For instance, there are far more ways to greet and socialize with people in Arabic than in English'.

When talking on the phone, Ruth is taken for an Egyptian. Sometimes her interlocutor asks where she comes from in Egypt to trace her accent, or they think she is an Egyptian living abroad. It's only when they see her that they realize she's not Arab at all. Ruth not only speaks like an Arab; she has also adopted their body language. Ruth explains, 'In Arabic you can say a lot without actually using language. When I speak Arabic, I become more expressive, and I use my hands a lot more'. Many of these gestures are culture-dependent, and they would not work in another language.

Even though Ruth tries not to mix languages, this is what many of her Egyptian friends do. Sometimes they do this for practical or cultural reasons. In a culture where sex is a taboo, women often switch to English when referring to the intimate parts of their body (in Arabic, these words are often used as swear words). On the other hand, some people want to show off with their English, which is often associated with higher class or good education. As in many other countries, people with money send their children to private English-language schools or universities. As a result, some Egyptians are actually more fluent in English than in Arabic.

Last but not least, Ruth draws attention to the fact that the insecurity of life takes a prominent position in the Arabic language. For instance, rather than answering a question with a yes or no, an Arab will say *inshallah* (إن شاء الله) which in English translates as 'God willing'. The phrase is used by everyone, even by non-believers, and it is used all over the Middle East. What it expresses is that one can never know for sure what life will bring tomorrow, which makes sense in a region torn apart by war and conflict. As Ruth points out, translating Arabic can be challenging. Depending on the context, *inshallah* can be translated as 'hopefully', but also as 'yes' or 'no'.

Unfortunately, a lot is lost in translation. 'Some things sound so beautiful in Arabic, but they don't mean anything in English', Ruth concludes.

Dodoma, Tanzania

It was really confusing.

(Edward M.)

Like most countries in Africa, Tanzania is highly multilingual. *Ethnologue* lists 127 languages, none of which is spoken by a majority of the population.[5] Within their own communities, Tanzania's various ethnic groups speak their mother tongues, while for communication with other communities, Swahili (also known as Kiswahili)[6] and English are widely used as lingua francas. Swahili is the official national language. Besides, it is the language of primary education as well as of the social and political sphere. English, the language inherited from British colonial rule (the British assumed control over the former German colony in 1920 as a result of the Treaty of Versailles) is the language of secondary and higher education, technology, and higher courts. The language barrier between primary and secondary education is a major issue, as many children have no prior knowledge of English. Private primary schools, in which English is the medium of instruction, are better than public schools, but also more expensive. Even though Tanzania is a former British colony, the level of English remains problematic. Many students as well as their lecturers are not able to learn or teach effectively in English.[7]

Edward M., a lecturer in development studies, is a speaker of Gogo (one of the many local languages, also known as Kigogo) as well as Swahili and English. His language history reflects the linguistic complexities the country has to cope with:

> I grew up in the rural countryside located in the central part of Tanzania. Both my parents belong to the same ethnic group called Wagogo. The Wagogo are semi-pastoral; they are involved in agriculture and livestock keeping. The language that I speak with my mother is Kigogo. Our national language is Kiswahili, which is used as a medium of instruction in primary schools. I remember my first attempt to learn this language was the day I enrolled in primary school. As pupils, we were encouraged to adopt Kiswahili as our language for learning and communication and to do away with our vernacular language, especially when we were at school compounds. The pupils spoke many different languages, and that's why they needed a common language. Kiswahili was the only common language. It is also the symbol of unification. In primary school, all subjects were taught in Kiswahili. In secondary school,

however, everything was in English. It's the official language and medium of instruction in both secondary schools and higher learning institutions in Tanzania. Thus for the first time, I learned English once I joined secondary school. Initially, it was very difficult for me to use English to learn similar subjects and concepts which had been taught in Kiswahili for seven years in primary school. It was really confusing. At one point in time I felt like translating concepts from Kiswahili to English instead of learning them in English. Science subjects such as biology, chemistry and physics were very tough because most of the jargon was new to me and varied a lot from what I used to learn in Kiswahili.

Currently, Edward attends a master's programme in development studies at a university in Europe. As all other students, Edward had to take an English language test prior to the start of the programme. Much to Edward's surprise, he failed the test, as a result of which he was required to attend an English language course while pursuing his master's degree in Europe.

Bujumbura, Burundi

I often mix languages.

(Riza H.)

Burundi was an independent kingdom until the beginning of the twentieth century, when the region was colonized by Germany. After Germany's defeat in the First World War, the territory was ceded to Belgium, which already had the Congo. Whereas the Germans had promoted the use of Swahili (the lingua franca of the wider region), the Belgians favoured Kirundi, which is spoken by the vast majority in Burundi. The fact that Burundi has a single indigenous language is unique in Africa. As a result of Belgian colonial rule, French plays an important role in government, business, and education.

Since 2014, Burundi has three official languages: Kirundi, French, and English. Swahili is mentioned as a fourth language, even though it does not have an official status. Kirundi is promoted by the government as a unifying language. It is mutually intelligible with Kinyarwanda, which is an official language in neighbouring Rwanda. Both form a dialect continuum known as Rwanda-Rundi. Although French is used as a language for wider communication, it is spoken by an educated minority only. The former colonial language is perceived as a 'necessary evil' (*un mal nécessaire*).[8] Because of the dominance of English worldwide and due to the fact that most countries in the region are English-speaking, Burundi felt encouraged to adopt English as an additional language. Its French-speaking neighbours Rwanda and Congo have pursued similar policies. Whereas French remains an important international language, English is the language of globalization.

Riza H. lives in Bujumbura, the capital of Burundi, where she is involved in a peace project aimed at conflict resolution and reconciliation in the Great Lakes region. Riza grew up with Kirundi and French. Like most people in Burundi, Riza's first language is Kirundi, but she was educated in French from primary school onwards. Moreover, she is a fluent speaker of English, which she started learning in secondary education. Apart from these three languages, she understands some Swahili, but she cannot speak it. I asked Riza what these languages mean to her, and what she associates them with.

> Kirundi is our national language … I think I dream in Kirundi and I use it for strong emotions. When I'm angry, I use my mother tongue. Kirundi is not used as a medium of instruction, but sometimes it is used at school to explain something or to make a joke, which is easier in your mother tongue. Kirundi is very important for my identity. When I'm abroad and I hear someone speak Kirundi, it's like I hear a brother or a sister. We share something. You establish some kind of relationship, and you get more opportunities, and even favours. When I was in Rwanda, for instance, I could speak with the people in the language we share. I felt like I was being accepted as a 'good person'. Kirundi and Kinyarwanda are not the same language, but they are very similar. The main difference is the accent. In Rwanda, I change my accent to be better understood, but people will notice immediately I'm from Burundi.
>
> French is the language of prestige. If you can speak French, you show you are an intellectual. It is the language of *les cultivés*, 'the civilized'. In the past, it was the only language we could speak with foreigners. Today we often use English.
>
> This is the twenty-first century, in which English is necessary. English is the language of the world. It's an advantage not to remain Francophone only. Contrary to Rwanda, where English was imposed top-down, the approach in Burundi has been more gradual. Yet the level of English remains rather low. Its use in higher education remains limited, except in private universities, which are English only.
>
> When I was a child, Kiswahili mainly had negative connotations, and my parents did not want me to use it. It was associated with 'bad people', dirt and poverty, and it was mainly spoken in suburbs, which is still the case in Bujumbura. Nowadays the connotations are more positive, especially in the context of East Africa, where the language is widely used.
>
> I often mix these languages. It's normal to do so. I rarely finish a sentence without changing languages. Sometimes it is even necessary because a word or concept does not exist in a language. For instance, there is no word for 'library' in Kirundi. When I say in Kirundi I go to the library, I have to use the French word for library: *Ngiye muri bibliothèque*.

4 Pacific

Rahui-Pōkeka, New Zealand

I'm finding my feet again.

(Taheke Noda)

The Māori are the indigenous inhabitants of New Zealand (Aotearoa), originating from Polynesia. The arrival of Europeans from the seventeenth century onwards changed the Māori way of life due to the dominance of Western culture. Currently, the Māori make up some 15 per cent of the population. The largest group consists of white New Zealanders, commonly referred to as *Pakeha* in Māori. The Māori language, an eastern Polynesian language, is also known as *te reo* ('the language'). Missionaries introduced the Latin alphabet in the nineteenth century, as Māori lacked an indigenous writing system. The number of Māori speakers has declined sharply since 1945, but due to language revitalization efforts, the language has witnessed a revival in recent years.

Taheke lives in Huntly (Rahui-Pōkeka in Māori), a town in the North Island of New Zealand and an area steeped in Māori history. White people call him Hex as they have troubles pronouncing his Māori name. As Taheke remarks, '*Pakeha* people in New Zealand can be very ignorant when it comes to trying to pronounce Māori names or places right'.

Taheke speaks English in everyday life and at work (he works as a plastic welder). Māori is the language he speaks at his *marae*, the 'meeting grounds' and the focal point of Māori communities. As Māori is the language of his *tupuna* (ancestors), he feels like he's representing his family. The language fills him with respect. He doesn't usually speak Māori around *Pakeha* people, but he speaks it with other Māori, who will not discriminate.

Although Taheke is more fluent in English than in Māori, the latter is very important for his identity. 'In the Māori language I'm finding my feet again', Taheke admits. Yet he didn't speak Māori for almost 16 years. When he was in his early twenties and left home, he didn't have anyone around to speak it to. In addition, as Taheke explains:

> I was trying to get familiar with the way *Pakeha* people act and talk to help me get a job, even to the point where I found myself dumbing down Māori words so they could understand what place I was talking about or which person I was talking about.

It was only last year he started speaking Māori again. This was at his father's *tangi* (traditional funeral), when he had to represent his immediate family. He had to do the same at his mum's and brother's *tangi*. 'This helped me get in touch with my Māori side again', Taheke adds.

Taheke wants to raise his 1-year-old daughter in both English and Māori. Sometimes he mixes both languages. For instance, when he is explaining something to his daughter, he might say, 'Come over here, *e noho*' (*e noho* means sit). Being Māori is very important for Taheke. He says, 'I'm working on getting my *ta moko* [Māori tattoo] on my body to represent my *maoritanga* even more' [*maoritanga*: Māori culture, traditions, and way of life].

5 Latin America

Managua, Nicaragua

> *English sounds better with some Spanish on it.*
>
> (Fernanda S.)

Nicaragua's multi-ethnic population includes people of indigenous, European, African, and Asian heritage. The country's main language is Spanish, a legacy of the Spanish colonization in the sixteenth century until 1821, when Nicaragua gained its independence. Since its independence, Nicaragua has undergone several periods of political unrest, leading to the Nicaraguan Revolution and the Contra War (1960s–1990s). In 1979, the left-wing Sandinistas[9] took power, ending 46 years of dictatorship of the Somoza family. The new government introduced social reform policies but they also nationalized the country's major industries, prompting he exodus of Nicaragua's middle class, many of whom settled in the United States. Various rebel groups (collectively known as the Contras) opposed the government with the support of the United States. The Contras engaged in a systematic campaign of terror, human rights violations, and economic sabotage. On the other hand, the Sandinistas have also been accused of human rights abuses, particularly towards peasants and the Miskito people.[10]

This background is important to understand the story of Fernanda S., a social scientist based in Managua. Apart from Spanish, her native language, she speaks Portuguese, a language she learned while living in Brazil as an adolescent and which she regards as her second language. She is also fluent in English, which she learned in high school and while living in the United States after the revolution in Nicaragua. This is her story:

> I grew up in Nicaragua during the 1980s. I learned to see the US as our enemy, the country that was financing the war against us. I was a child, but I have vivid recollections of the toll of war and the economic embargo in our daily lives. During the early 1990s, after the revolution, my family sent me to the US to learn English (I had already taken courses in high school). They thought it was fundamental for me to learn that language if I wanted to do better in life (get a job, etc.). While they were right (knowing English has been an asset), their decision seemed so contradictory to me. At that time, I did not mention anything to them, and I did not rebel either. I went along with it but, initially, I rejected speaking the language. I felt guilty about

being in the US, about speaking the language; in my mind I was betraying Nicaragua – I was 'siding' with the enemy.

I also rejected having friendships with people from the US. I feared them. I lived in a southern state of the US and unequal racial relationships only added fuel to my rejection of the US, in particular of white America. It took me years, and meeting very loving people, to change my view of the language. I do not regret having learned it. I enjoy it now. I just feel it took a while for me to come to terms with the fact that the power relationships between countries do not reflect how all people from those countries are and how they relate to each other.

In this story, it is important to take into account that I actually left Nicaragua and went to the US to learn the language and that my family had the resources to send me. When I was in high school I did not reject learning English, I thought it was cool to learn another language and I wanted to learn as many more languages as I could. I do not have any recollection of meeting people from the US during my childhood, yet I didn't fear or reject 'foreigners' from Europe. It was in the 1990s that I met a lot of people from the US who supported the revolution in Nicaragua and who did amazing things to try to stop the war financed by their own country.

I did associate English with imperialism. And it was other people who changed my view of that. I guess one could say globalization helped to the extent that my presence in the US was part of the flows and movement of people and goods linked to globalization. But fundamentally, it was getting to meet people who expressed respect towards Nicaragua and other places in the world that allowed me to break down many prejudices. By the way, it was very important in my own relationship with the language to meet Latinos/Hispanics/Mexican Americans/Puerto Ricans who appropriated the language and mixed English with Spanish. To me, English always sounds much better with some Spanish on it.

Camagüey, Cuba

English is like the dollar.

(Enrique G.)

In spite of its being a multi-ethnic country whose people derive from diverse origins in the Americas, Europe, and Africa, Cuba is fairly homogeneous from a linguistic point of view in that Spanish is spoken as a first language by the vast majority of the population. Cuba was a Spanish colony from the fifteenth century until the Spanish–American War (1898), when the island was occupied by the United States. It gained nominal independence as a de facto US protectorate in 1902. Mounting unrest and social strife led to the dictatorship of Fulgencio Batista (1952–1959), a corrupt and oppressive regime backed by the United States. Batista was ousted by the 26th of July Movement, which later established communism under the leadership of Fidel Castro. As a consequence, Cuba was at the centre of the Cold War between the United States and the Soviet Union, which almost brought the world to the brink of nuclear war in 1962. After the collapse of the Soviet Union in 1989, Cuba could no longer depend on Moscow for aid. The ensuing 'Special Period' (*Periodo especial*) led to an extended economic crisis, as a result of which Cuba had to take some market-oriented measures to boost the economy. For instance, private initiatives such as *casa particulares* ('rooms for tourists') were approved. However, even today, in the post-Castro era, most Cubans have a hard life to make ends meet. Moreover, the United States embargo against Cuba – a series of commercial, economic, and financial sanctions which were first imposed in 1958 – has not been lifted yet. In Cuba, the embargo is called *el bloqueo* ('the blockade'), which reveals their view on the sanctions.

Enrique G. is a Cuban lawyer who works as a private taxi driver. Driving a cab is more lucrative than being a lawyer in Cuba, especially if one works in the tourist sector. This is also the sector in which English is needed, a language which is not widely spoken by most ordinary Cubans. In fact, English is hardly spoken at all in Cuba, even though the government decided to turn learning English into a priority in their education system. This is a striking contrast with the Cold War era, when Russian used to be the most popular language in Cuba. Learning English was not encouraged at all, and it was even seen as 'supporting the Americans'.[11] In today's Cuba, however, Russian has long lost its prominent position to English, which is increasingly seen as a means to gain access to the world.[12]

'English is like the dollar', Enrique explains during a five-hour drive from Camagüey to Trinidad. That is, English opens doors, and wallets as well. Although Enrique learned some English while studying at university, he picked up a lot more afterwards when dealing with foreigners. Enrique vividly remembers the days when having contacts with foreigners was considered as not being *revolucionario*, which could have severe consequences (e.g. losing your job). Even contacts with Cuban relatives living abroad were virtually forbidden until the mid-1990s. Enrique's cab, a classic American that takes you back in time, doubles as his classroom. Although his English language skills are quite limited, he manages to get across his message.

Enrique's ultimate dream is to leave Cuba, a dream he shares with many other Cubans. The only foreign country Enrique ever visited is Angola, where he served as a soldier. Like tens of thousands of other Cubans, Enrique fought in the Angolan Civil War (1975–2002), in which Cuba supported the leftist government against US-backed interventions. Under the Castro regime, Cuba was heavily involved in wars in Africa, Central America, and Asia. After his return from Angola, Enrique went to university to become a lawyer in Cuba, a job he quit after some 20 years as his income was not sufficient to support his family. As Enrique explains, most professionals in Cuba are paid in Cuban pesos (a currency whose value is 25 times lower than the Cuban convertible peso, also known as CUC), while nearly all consumer goods are sold in CUC. As a *chofer privado* ('private driver'), Enrique can stock up on hard currency CUCs.

Enrique's story is not very different from that of many other Cuban intellectuals, including medical doctors or university professors, whose wage does not allow them to make a decent living. English is the access to making more money, and many of those who are proficient in English, for instance teachers of English, quit their teaching jobs and set up business in the far more lucrative tourist business, where they can earn a month's wage in a single day. English sells, and it sells well.

6 Europe

Mitrovica, Kosovo

It is something that I represent.

(Arber Hoti)

Kosovo (Kosova in Albanian) is a partially recognized state in former Yugoslavia. It is bordered by Serbia to the north and east, North Macedonia to the south-east, Albania to the south-west, and Montenegro to the west. The Battle of Kosovo (1389) between the Serbs and the Ottomans remains an important *lieu de mémoire* for Serbian nationalism (see Chapter 7). Throughout the twentieth century, there have been tensions between the Albanian majority and the Serb minority in Kosovo. In 2008, Kosovo declared its independence from Serbia, where the Serbs are the majority. Serbia does not recognize Kosovo as a sovereign state, but as an 'autonomous province' within Serbia. Albanian and Serbian are official languages in Kosovo, while Bosnian, Turkish, and Romani are recognized regional languages.

Arber speaks Albanian as his first language. It is the language he speaks in everyday life with his family and friends. In addition, he is quite fluent in English, the language he learned at school and which he uses almost every day for professional reasons (Arber works for an international documentary film festival in Prizren). Arber picked up Turkish from television and he can speak some Serbian as well ('but not very good', he quickly adds). When I asked him whether he knew Russian too, he replied, 'Russian we don't speak here and we don't learn it at school'. In fact, Russian was no longer taught in Yugoslavia after 1948, when Tito and Stalin ended their friendship. While Serbian and Russian are Slavic languages, Albanian is not closely related to any other language in Europe.

Like other regions in former Yugoslavia, multi-ethnic Kosovo is a melting pot of languages, which are often mixed. For example, someone might say, '*Gidiyorum opstinama me mar ni dokument*', which is a mixture of Turkish (*gidiyorum*), Serbian (*opstinama*) and Albanian (the rest of the sentence). In English, the sentence reads, 'I'm going to the municipalities to get a document'. It's not something Arber would say, though.

Arber was born in 1989, the year in which Serbian leader Slobodan Milošević delivered his infamous speech on the site of the Battle of Kosovo. Even though the speech has been linked to the bloodshed in the ensuing wars, it appears to be a thing of the past for Arber. As he admits, 'I don't know anything about the speech'. In spite of this, he claims that the war in Kosovo (1998–1999) means a lot to him. After the war, when Arber was still a teenager, he lived with his family in North Mitrovica, a region with an ethnic Serb majority in the north of Kosovo, not far from Serbia. Arber remembers it was dangerous to speak Albanian in those days as the Serbs might attack them if they found out they were Kosovo Albanians. This is what actually happened to many speakers of Albanian who lived in the north of the city.

Today Mitrovica is divided between an Albanian and a Serbian part, and the bridge which links (and separates) both sides of the city is guarded by NATO soldiers. For both Albanians and Serbs, the other part of their city is a no-go zone. The two parts of the city look increasingly different, with different languages and scripts, flags, monuments, currencies, car number plates, and even graffiti.

Arber admits that there are many people in Kosovo (and in other parts of former Yugoslavia) who don't like the Serbs because of what they did during the war, but he doesn't have negative feelings as 'not all Serbs were in the war and not all of them supported the Serbian army'. Nevertheless, Arber believes his Albanian language and identity to be very important – 'it is something that I represent', he adds. He also admits that Albanians are very nationalistic when it comes to things such as their flag, language, and territory.

Aarhus, Denmark

English is an easy language to speak with foreigners.

(Oona Van Achter)

Denmark is one of the most affluent countries in the world. Moreover, it ranks in the top five of countries with a very high proficiency of English.[13] Denmark shares this position with some other Scandinavian countries and the Netherlands. Even though English is not an official language, it features prominently in education as well as in daily life. Like many other Western countries, Denmark has witnessed a steady increase in immigration from non-Western countries in the last decades, posing tremendous challenges to the country as it is being faced with new multilingual and multicultural realities.

Oona is a medical student at the University of Aarhus. As a native speaker of Danish, she has almost full understanding of Swedish and Norwegian as well. However, she adds, 'When I talk to a Swede, he or she often speaks Swedish to me and I respond in Danish. I do the same with Norwegians. When Danish is not an option, my second choice of language is mostly English'. Apart from English, which she speaks and writes fluently, she knows Dutch, as well as some German and French. The latter two remain limited to small talk such as ordering a drink in a bar.

While her mother tongue is Danish – it literally is the language she speaks with her mother – her father's language is Dutch. Her father, who lives in Belgium, always speaks Dutch to her. In a conversation with her father, Oona speaks Danish and he speaks Dutch. This is another instance of *translanguaging*, which is possible because she understands Dutch and he understands Danish. When I asked Oona whether she considers herself a Danish–Dutch bilingual, she replied:

> I consider myself a Danish person who can also, to some degree, speak Dutch because my father has always spoken Dutch to me. To consider myself a Danish–Dutch bilingual I think my spoken (and written) Dutch would need to improve a lot. So far, I have always preferred speaking Danish rather than Dutch. I associate Danish with everything in my daily life – communication with the people around me, studying, writing, working, etc. In fact, I do not associate Danish with very specific things because Danish is present in my life all the time and I do not think about it when I use it or hear it. Dutch, on the other hand, I very much associate with holidays in Belgium where I for example listen to Flemish radio stations (and think about the language or some words I don't know), read the Dutch signs on the highway, speak to people. When I am in Belgium, I use Dutch with everybody else than my father as he understands Danish. I use Dutch with the friends of my father, at the supermarket, at cafés etc. This is mainly to practise my Dutch as I actually feel more confident speaking English instead of Dutch.

At what age did you realize Danish and Dutch are different languages?

> Maybe around the age of 5. I was at the airport in Brussels and I realized that nobody understood what I was saying in Danish, but I managed to communicate a little in Dutch. After that I think I understood that Danish and Dutch were different languages.

When she was an adolescent, Oona was hesitant to speak Dutch, and she preferred to speak English. When I asked her when and why she switched to Dutch, she answered:

> I am not sure when it was as I don't remember it that clearly. Maybe it is five or ten years ago? But I guess I was not at all confident speaking Dutch because I knew that I was not able to speak it correctly. Furthermore, I was not able to be a part of a discussion because my Dutch vocabulary is relatively limited and speaking English was just easier. Not that my English is perfect, but English is an easy language to speak with foreigners who do not speak it as a first language either. You can meet at almost the same level of linguistic skills and everybody can more easily be part of the conversation. When I got older, I realized that I had to speak Dutch to become good at it and I felt more confident doing so – with or without language mistakes. I can still feel very limited when I want to make a point in Dutch because I know exactly what to say in Danish, but I don't know the Dutch words or I do not have them present in my memory. If the discussion were in Danish (or in English) it would be easier for me to express my opinions. Sometimes I use English words

in my Dutch when I don't know the word in Dutch. When I talk to people from the Netherlands, I can often sense that they try to place my accent or dialect and they are trying to figure out whether I am from Belgium or not.

Last but not least, I asked Oona whether she regards language as part of her identity. She replied:

> Very much, I think! Maybe language is not directly a part of my identity, but it is my way to communicate who I am and my instrument to express myself, my thoughts and my opinions to other people. Danish and Dutch, as well as Denmark and Belgium for that matter, represent elements that I use to define myself.

Notes

1 See: www.ethnologue.com/18/language/ifk/ (accessed 22 November 2018).
2 See: www.ethnologue.com/language/mar (accessed 27 November 2018).
3 In a recent speech (2 January 2019), Chinese president Xi Jinping claimed that Taiwan 'must and will be' reunited with China. See: www.bbc.com/news/world-asia-china-46733174 (accessed 9 January 2019).
4 Pinyin is the official Romanization system for Standard Chinese in mainland China and to some extent in Taiwan.
5 See: www.ethnologue.com/country/tz (accessed 28 September 2018).
6 While in English the language is commonly referred to as Swahili, my interviewee uses the term Kiswahili (with the ki-prefix to refer to the language). The same holds for Gogo and Kigogo. The ethnic group is called Wagogo.
7 Kjølstad Gran (2007). See: www.duo.uio.no/bitstream/handle/10852/30959/ LineKjolstadGran%5B1%5D.pdf?sequence=1 (accessed 5 December 2018).
8 See: www.axl.cefan.ulaval.ca/afrique/burundi.htm (in French) (accessed 26 November 2018).
9 The Sandinistas took their name from César Augusto Sandino, a hero of the resistance to US military occupation (1927–1933).
10 The Miskito are an indigenous ethnic group. They speak a native Miskito language, but many also speak creole English or Spanish. Creole English is the result of frequent trade contacts with the British.
11 Pignatelli (2016).
12 Vyas (2015). See: www.wsj.com/articles/cubans-say-nyet-to-russian-hoping-to-learn-english-1448044268 (accessed 2 July 2018).
13 See: www.ef.com/wwen/epi/ (accessed 2 May 2019).

REFERENCES

Acemoglu, Daron and Robinson, James A. (2013) *Why Nations Fail. The Origins of Power, Prosperity, and Poverty*. London: Profile.
Anderson, Benedict (1983) *Imagined Communities. Reflections on the Origin and Spread of Nationalism* (revised ed.). London: Verso.
Armstrong, C.A.J. (1965, 1983) 'The Language Question in the Low Countries: The Use of French and Dutch by the Dukes of Burgundy and Their Administration', in J.R. Hale, J. Highfield, and B. Smalley (Eds.), *Europe in the Late Middle Ages*. London: Faber & Faber, pp. 386–409.
Baker, Paul (2004) *Fantabulosa: A Dictionary of Polari and Gay Slang*. London: Bloomsbury.
Barnes, Julian (2013) *Levels of Life*. London: Vintage.
Bauman, Richard and Briggs, Charles L. (2003) *Voices of Modernity. Language Ideologies and the Politics of Modernity*. Cambridge: Cambridge University Press.
Billig, Michael (1995) *Banal Nationalism*. London: SAGE.
Blommaert, Jan (2010) *The Sociolinguistics of Globalization*. London: John Benjamins.
Bourdieu, Pierre (1991) *Language and Symbolic Power*. Cambridge: Polity Press.
Boye, Sarah (2016) *Intercultural Communicative Competence and Short Stays Abroad. Perceptions of Development*. Munster: Waxman.
Canetti, Elias (1987) *Das Geheimherz der Uhr. Aufzeichnungen 1973–1985*. Berlin: Hanser.
Chakrabarty, Dipesh (2000) *Provincializing Europe. Postcolonial Thought and Historical Difference*. Princeton, NJ: Princeton University Press.
Chomsky, Noam (1957) *Syntactic Structure*. The Hague/Paris: Mouton.
Classen, C., Howes, D., and Synnott, A. (1994) *Aroma. The Cultural History of Smell*. New York: Routledge.
Coleman, M.C. (2010) 'You Might All Be Speaking Swedish Today. Language Change in 19th Century Finland and Ireland'. *Scandinavian Journal of History*, 35, 1, 44–64.
Crawford, James (1995) 'Endangered Native American Languages. What Is to Be Done, and Why?'. *The Bilingual Research Journal*, 19, 1, 17–38.
Crystal, David (2003) *English as a Global Language*. Cambridge: Cambridge University Press.
Dalby, Andrew (2002) *Language in Danger. How Language Loss Threatens Our Future*. London: Penguin.

Darwin, Charles (1859, 1987) *The Origin of Species by Means of Natural Selection or the Preservation of Favoured Races in the Struggle for Life*. London: Penguin.

De Grauwe, Luc (1999) *Welke taal sprak Keizer Karel?* Bussum: Spiegel Historiael.

De Grauwe, Luc (2004) 'Zijn *Olla Vogala* Vlaams, of zit de Nederlandse filologie met een koekoeksei in (haar) nest(en)?'. *TNTL*, 120, 44–56.

de Rivarol, Antoine (1784, 1995) *De l'universalité européenne de la langue française*. Paris: Librairie Arthème Fayard.

De Swaan, Abram (2001) *Words of the World. The Global Language System*. Malden, MA: Polity Press.

Dil, Anwar S. (Ed.) (1972) *The Ecology of Language. Essays by Einar Haugen*. Stanford, CA: Stanford University Press.

Duchêne, Alexandre and Heller, Monica (2007) *Discourses of Endangerement. Ideology and Interest in the Defence of Languages*. London: Continuum.

Eberhard, David M., Simons, Gary F., and Fennig, Charles D. (Eds.) (2019) *Ethnologue: Languages of the World* (22nd ed.). Dallas, TX: SIL International.

Edwards, Alison (2016) *English in the Netherlands. Function, Forms and Attitude*. Amsterdam: John Benjamins.

Evans, Vyvyan (2016) *The Language Myth*. Cambridge: Cambridge University Press.

Flesch, R.F. (1944) 'How Basic is Basic English?'. *Harper's Magazine*, March, pp. 339–343.

Galeano, Eduardo (1971/1997) *Open Veins of Latin America. Five Centuries of the Pillage of a Continent*. London: Profile.

Gat, Azar and Yakobson, Alexander (2013) *Nations. The Long History of Political Ethnicity and Nationalism*. Cambridge: Cambridge University Press.

Gellner, Ernest (1983) *Nations and Nationalism* (2nd ed.). Blackwell: Oxford.

Gill, Saran Kaur and Kirkpatrick, Andy (2013) 'English in Asian and European Higher Education', in C.A. Chapelle (Ed.), *The Encyclopedia of Applied Linguistics*. Oxford: Wiley-Blackwell, pp. 1916–1920.

Glenny, Misha (1996) *The Fall of Yugoslavia*. London: Penguin.

Groeneboer, K. (1988) *Gateway to the West. The Dutch Language in Colonial Indonesia 1600–1950*. Amsterdam: Amsterdam University Press.

Habash, Nizar Y. (2010) *Introduction to Arabic Natural Language Processing*. San Rafael, CA: Morgan & Claypool.

Harari, Yuval Noah (2017) *Homo Deus. A Brief History of Tomorrow*. London: Penguin.

Haugen, Einar (1972) 'The Ecology of Language'. *The Linguistic Reporter*, 25, 19–26.

Haugen, Einar (1987) *Blessings of Babel. Bilingualism and Language Planning. Problems and Pleasures*. New York: Mouton de Gruyter.

Hultgren, A.K., Gregersen, F., and Thøgersen, J. (Eds.) (2014) *English in Nordic Universities. Ideologies and Practices*. Amsterdam: John Benjamins.

Huntington, Samuel (1996) *The Clash of Civilizations and the Remaking of World Order*. New York: Simon & Schuster.

Hutton, Christopher M. (2001) *Linguistics and the Third Reich. Mother-Tongue Fascism, Race and the Science of Language*. London: Routledge.

Jenkins, Jennifer (2009) 'English as a Lingua Franca: Interpretations and Attitudes'. *World Englishes*, 28, 2, 200–207.

Joseph, John E. (2006) *Language and Politics*. Edinburgh: Edinburgh University Press.

Kachru, Braj B. (1985) 'Standards, Codification and Sociolinguistic Realism: The English Language in the Outer Circle', in R. Quirk and H. Widdowson (Eds.), *English in the World. Teaching and Learning the Language and Literatures*. Cambridge: Cambridge University Press, pp. 11–36.

Kachru, Braj B. (2005) *Asian Englishes. Beyond the Canon*. Hong Kong: Hong Kong University Press.

Khan, Abdul Jamil (2006) *Urdu/Hindi. An Artificial Divide*. New York: Algora.
Kirby, David (2006) *A Concise History of Finland*. Cambridge: Cambridge University Press.
Kjølstad Gran, Line (2007) *Language of Instruction in Tanzanian Higher Education*. Masters Thesis, University of Oslo.
Kloss, Heinz (1967) '"Abstand" Languages and "Ausbau" Languages'. *Anthropological Linguistics*, 9, 7, 29–41.
Knight, Kathtryn (2015) 'Orangutans Use Hand Like Soundbox to Make Alarm Calls'. *Journal of Experimental Biology*, 218, 813.
Krauss, Nicole (2005) *The History of Love*. London: Penguin.
Kuteeva, M. (2014) 'The Parallel Language Use of Swedish and English. The Question of "Nativeness" in University Policies and Practices'. *Journal of Multilingual and Multicultural Development*, 35, 4, 332–334.
Lakoff, George and Johnson, Mark (1980) *Metaphors We Live By*. Chicago, IL: University of Chicago Press.
Lawton, Rachele (2013) 'Speak English or Go Home: The Anti-Immigrant Discourse of the "English Only" Movement'. *CADAAD*, 7, 1, 100–122.
Linden, Eugene (1987) *Silent Partners. The Legacy of the Ape Language Experiments*. New York: Ballantine.
Malcolm, Noel (1998) *Kosovo. A Short Story*. London: Macmillan.
Mauldin, Laura (2016) *Made to Hear. Cochlear Implants and Raising Deaf Children*. Minneapolis, MN: University of Minneapolis Press.
May, Stephen (2006) 'Language Policy and Minority Rights', in T. Ricento (Ed.), *An Introduction to Language Policy. Theory and Method*. London: Blackwell, pp. 255–272.
McLean, Iain and McMillan, Alistair (2003) *Concise Dictionary of Politics*. Oxford: Oxford University Press.
Mills, Kenneth and Taylor, William B. (1988) *Colonial Spanish America. A Documentary History*. Lanham, MD: Rowman & Littlefield.
Mudde, Cas (2007) *Populist Radical Right Parties in Europe*. Cambridge: Cambridge University Press.
Mufwene, Salikoko S. (2004) 'Language Birth and Death'. *Annual Review of Anthropology*, 33, 201–222.
Mugane, John M. (2015) *The Story of Swahili*. Athens, OH: Ohio University Press.
Norda, Pierre (1996) *Realms of Memory. The Construction of the French Past*. New York: Columbia University Press.
Nović, Sara (2018a) 'A Clearer Message on Cochlear Implants'. *New York Times*, 21 November.
Nović, Sara (2018b) *Girl at War*. London: Abacus.
Or, Iair G. and Shohamy, Elana (2016) 'Asymmetries and Inequalities in the Teaching of Arabic and Hebrew in the Israeli Educational System'. *Journal of Language and Politics*, 15, 1, 25–44.
Orwell, George (1945) *Animal Farm*. London: Secker & Warburg.
Orwell, George (1946) *Politics and the English Language*. London: Penguin.
Orwell, George (1949) *Nineteen Eighty-Four*. London: Penguin.
Ostler, Nicholas (2006) *Empires of the Word. A Language History of the World*. London: Harper.
Painter, Desmond William (2010) *Tongue Tied. The Politics of Language, Subjectivity and Social Psychology in South Africa*. PhD Dissertation, University of South Africa.
Pennycook, Alastair (2006) 'Postmodernism in Language Policy', in T. Ricento (Ed.), *An Introduction to Language Policy. Theory and Method*. London: Blackwell, pp. 60–76.
Pennycook, Alastair (2018) *Posthumanist Applied Linguistics*. London: Routledge.
Pepperberg, Irene (2002) *The Alex Studies: Cognitive and Communicative Abilities of Grey Parrots*. Cambridge MA: Harvard University Press.

Phillipson, Robert (1992) *Linguistic Imperialism*. Oxford: Oxford University Press.
Pignatelli, Beatrice (2016) 'English Language Learning in Cuba'. *Havana Times*, 27 January.
Pinker, Steven (1994) *The Language Instinct. How the Mind Creates Language*. London: Penguin.
Saarinen, Tania (2012) 'Internationalization of Finnish Higher Education. Is Language an Issue?'. *IJSL*, 216, 157–173.
Savski, Kristof (2016) 'Analysing Voice in Language Policy. Plurality and Conflict in Slovene Government Documents'. *Language Policy*, 15, 4, 505–524.
Schneider, Edgar (2007) *Postcolonial English: Varieties around the World*. Cambridge: Cambridge University Press.
Sebba, Mark (2007) *Spelling and Society. The Culture and Politics of Orthography around the World*. Cambridge: Cambridge University Press.
Shell, Marc (2002) *American Babel*. Cambridge, MA: Harvard University Press.
Skutnabb-Kangas, Tove (2000) *Linguistic Genocide in Education – or Worldwide Diversity and Human Rights?* London: Lawrence Erlbaum.
Smith, Anthony D. (1991) *National Identity*. Harmondsworth: Penguin.
Spencer, Herbert (1864) *The Principles of Biology*. London: Williams & Norgate.
Spolsky, Bernard (2004) *Language Policy*. Cambridge: Cambridge University Press.
Spolsky, Bernard (2014) *The Languages of the Jews: A Sociolinguistic History*. Cambridge: Cambridge University Press.
Stibbe, Arran (2015) *Ecolinguistics. Language, Ecology, and the Stories We Live By*. London: Routledge.
Sudjic, Deyan (2017) *The Language of Cities*. London: Penguin.
Swales, John (1997) 'English as Tyrannosaurus Rex'. *World Englishes*, 16, 3, 373–382.
Tupas, Ruani and Salonga, Alleen (2016) 'Unequal Englishes'. *Journal of Sociolinguistics*, 20, 3, 367–381.
Van Dijk, Teun (1998) *Ideology. A Multidisciplinary Approach*. London: SAGE.
Van Splunder, Frank (2016) 'Language Ideologies Regarding English-Medium Instruction in European Higher Education. Insights from Flanders and Finland', in E. Barakos and J.W. Unger (Eds.), *Discursive Approaches to Language Policy*. London: Palgrave Macmillan, pp. 205–230.
Vertovec, Steven (2007) 'Superdiversity and Its Implications'. *Ethnic and Racial Studies*, 29, 6, 1024–1054.
von Clausewitz, Carl (1832, 1989) *On War*. Edited and translated by Michael Eliot Howard and Peter Paret. Princeton, NJ: Princeton University Press.
Vyas, Keyal (2015) 'Cubans Say "Nyet" to Russian, Hoping to Learn English'. *Wall Street Journal*, 22 November.
Wächter, Bernd and Maiworm, Manfred (2014) *English-Taught Programmes in European Higher Education*. Bonn: Lemmens.
Whitehead, Hal and Rendall, Luke (2015) *The Cultural Lives of Whales and Dolphins*. Chicago, IL: University of Chicago Press.
Widdowson, Henry G. (1994) 'The Ownership of English'. *TESOL Quarterly*, 28, 2, 377–389.
Witte, Els and Van Velthoven, Harry (1999) *Language and Politics. The Belgian Case Study in a Historical Perspective*. Brussels: VUB University Press.
Woolf, Virginia (1922) *Jacob's Room*. London: Hogarth.
Wulf, Andrea (2015) *The Invention of Nature. The Adventures of Alexander von Humboldt. The Lost Hero of Science*. London: Murray.
Yu, Yun and Moskal, Marta (2019) 'Missing Intercultural Engagements in the University Experiences of Chinese International Students in the UK'. *Compare: A Journal of Comparative and International Education*, 49, 4, 654–671.

INDEX

Abstand 38, 39, 49
Académie française 4, 7, 30, 39, 41, 46, 55
accent 6, 9, 64, 70, 116–17, 118, 121, 129; adaptation 33–4, 71–2
Africa 48, 50, 52, 55, 62, 73, 94, 96, 112, 117–23, 125
African Americans 18; languages 48, 50; slaves 33
Afrikaans 36–7, 38, 60, 94; Afrikaners 7, 37
Air France 73
Albanian 42, 82, 126–7
Algeria 84
Allah 102; *inshallah* 118–19
alphabet 40–3; Cyrillic 39, 57; Latin 39, 42, 58, 103, 122; revolution 42
ALTE 75
Anderson, Benedict 6, 25–7, 30
Angola 33, 58, 125
animal talk 21–3; animals vs humans 10, 16–17, 21–3, 27, 101–2, 106; apes 22–3, 102; bees 23; birds 10, 13, 22–3, 101; whales 22; wolves 16, 23
apartheid 7, 37, 60, 87, 94
Arabic 38, 44, 50, 52, 56, 61, 74, 81, 82, 84, 98, 104, 117–19; language of Islam 53, 56; script 42–3, 56, 59, 103
Aruhuaco 61–2
Asia 48, 50, 53, 54, 55, 56, 61, 62, 73, 75, 89, 94, 96, 112, 113–17, 125
Atatürk 42–3
atheism 92
Ausbau 38, 39, 49

Babel, Tower of 13, 32
Babylonia 77
Bahasa Indonesia 59
Balkans 81, 85
Bantu languages 33

barbarism 46
Basic English 20–1
Basque 84, 98
Battista, Fulgencio 124
Belgium 6, 41, 68, 85–8, 128–9; languages 5, 7, 8, 38, 39, 41, 55, 57, 60, 90, 97
Bengali 50, 52, 59, 60, 69; Bangladesh 60, 69, 73
Bible 28, 48
Big Brother 21
bilingualism 52, 86, 90, 128
black culture 11, 33
Blackbird Field 82
Blair, Tony 34
BMW 73
Bologna Declaration 75
book printing 27
Bosnian 39, 81, 85
Bourdieu, Pierre 7, 75, 103; *Language and Symbolic Power* 75
Boyle, Robert 68
Braille 32
Brazil 73
Brexit 54
British Council 75, 89; Empire 39, 49, 53, 59, 64, 67, 118; English 8, 23, 40, 74; Rover 73; Sign Language 18
Burundi 57, 112, 120–1

calligraphy 103
Camus, Albert 7
Canada 52, 53, 55, 99
Canetti, Elias 95
Cantonese 54, 60, 84
capitalism 28, 53; global academic capitalism 75; print capitalism 25
Castilian 55, 84; *see also* Spanish
Castro, Fidel 125

Catalan 31, 55, 72
Catalonia 6, 26, 31, 99, 108
Chan, Kai L. 51
characters (Chinese) 43, 54, 58, 103, 108
Charles V. 6–7
Charter for Regional and Minority Languages 31
China 7, 8, 10–11, 104, 116–17; economy 52, 54, 68; education 74; map 108; People's Republic 43
Chinese: imagined community 38; language 8, 10–11, 50, 52–3, 54, 61, 68, 74, 117; people 7, 43, 75, 77; writing system 42
Chinese English 70, 104
Chomsky, Noam 14–15, 22, 23, 106
Christianity 28, 48, 53, 92, 102, 103, 117
class 87, 88, 103, 117, 118, 123; class struggle 44; social class 5, 10, 25, 33, 34, 95, 114–15
Clausewitz, Carl von 79
cochlear implant 18
Cockney 34
code-switching 32
Cold War 52, 125
collateral damage 4
Collegium Trilingue 68
Colombia 32, 41, 55, 61, 62; Columbia 41; Columbus 41
colonization 40–1, 49–50, 55, 57–60, 61, 67, 73, 94, 98, 103, 111, 113, 123; colonies 25, 32, 69, 84, 89, 96, 104, 116, 119, 124; colonial languages 50, 55, 59, 60, 73, 84, 94, 96, 120
Commonwealth 39
communism 21, 28, 39, 40, 76, 116; China 43, 54, 116; Cuba 125; Yugoslavia 39
Congo 33, 55, 74, 94, 120
conquistadores 27, 55
Council of Europe 31
Creator 92
creole 58, 93–4
Croatian 39; Croatia 81
Cuba 44, 57, 74, 83, 124–6
cultural intelligence 15
Cyrillic *see* alphabet

Danish 3, 33, 38, 127–9; Denmark 3, 57, 127–9
Darwin, Charles 14, 15, 29, 92–3, 105
deaf 17, 18–19, 32; Deaf community 18, 20, 107
dialect 6, 10; animals 22–3; Chinese 54; continuum 56, 61, 113, 120; sign language 18; vs language 4, 9, 10, 17, 26–7, 36–8, 49, 51, 86

Dictionary of the Revolution 82–3
disability 18, 46
Disney, Walt 72, 77
Dodoma 119
Dutch 3, 8, 13, 127–9; Dutch Language Union 39; in Belgium 5, 8, 39, 86–7, 97; in colonies 59, 60, 89, 96; in the Netherlands 50, 60, 73, 76, 127–9; vs Afrikaans 36, 38, 94; vs English 37, 71, 76; vs German 6, 37–8, 70, 109; spelling 41

ecology 9, 28, 29, 95 105–8; ecological linguistics 105
education 7, 16, 30, 75, 77, 107–8; commodification of education 104; education system 26, 39, 112, 125; language of education 36, 87, 88
Edwards, Alison 95
Egypt 27, 56, 82–3, 101, 117–18
Einstein, Albert 64
England 29, 30, 31, 38, 61, 68, 94, 95
English 8, 19, 30, 34, 39, 50–2, 53–4, 104; as a lingua franca 18, 32, 53, 70, 71, 104, 107, 108, 109, 119; as a world language 9, 49, 67–71; communicative value 63, 108; English Only movement 56, 72, 74, 89, 90, 121; *hypercentral* language 61–2, 68, 103; in business 72–3; in education 59, 69, 74–7, 117; in France 30, 42, 64, 67, 84, 104; in South Africa 94; in the Netherlands 76; New Englishes 74, 94; ownership of English 70; prestige 57, 106, 112, 113, 115; spelling 40, 41; threat to other languages 7, 10, 42, 46, 84, 88, 90
Englishization 76
Enlightenment 28–9, 64
Erasmus 68
Eskimo 3, 16; *see also* Inuit
Esperanto 17, 19–20, 38
essentialism 29
ethnic cleansing 80
Ethnologue 19, 48, 52, 95, 113, 119
Europe 4, 26, 27, 30, 32, 48, 52, 63, 76, 84, 86, 96, 98, 103–4, 108
European higher education 75, 77; languages 5, 19, 25, 29, 30, 38, 50, 55, 56, 57, 61, 64; Parliament 74; Union 6, 54, 62
Evans, Vyvyan 15
evolution 14–15, 23, 29, 92–3, 95

Fawlty Towers 72
Filipino 113
final solution 80

Finland 7, 30, 76, 88; Finnish 76, 88
Flanders 5, 8, 26, 30, 37, 39, 41, 86–8, 97;
  Flemish nationalism 87; *see also* Dutch
Flesch, Rudolf 21
France 30, 31, 38, 55, 61, 63, 64, 73, 86; use
  of English 42, 46, 64, 67, 72
Franco 31, 84, 98, 99
Francophonie 30, 39, 84, 89, 121
French: language 6, 8, 10, 55, 73–4, 84, 120–1;
  language policy 29, 84, 86–7, 89, 97, 104;
  mission civilisatrice 60; normative tradition
  30; Rationalism 10, 28, 29; Revolution
  29, 44; spelling reform 41; supercentral
  language 63–4; universality 29
Frenchification 67, 84, 88, 97, 104
Frenchness 29, 31
Freud, Siegmund 71
Frisian 37
FYROM 31

Gaelic 98; Manx 31; Scottish 97
Galeano, Eduardo 55
Galician 55, 58
Galilei, Galileo 68
Gandhi, Mahatma 59
Gat, Azar 27
Gellner, Ernest 27
gender 5, 8, 17, 25, 32, 44–5, 95
German Democratic Republic 40
Germanic languages 6, 8, 19, 37
German language 6, 8, 37–8, 41, 43–4,
  52, 57, 67, 71, 74, 76, 89, 95, 127;
  Romanticism 28–9
Germany 30, 31, 63–4, 72, 73, 87; former
  colonies 119, 120
Globalization 3, 25, 52, 53–4, 61, 70, 75, 77,
  96, 103, 104, 106–8, 112, 114, 120, 124
Global Language System 61–3
God 13, 15, 27, 92, 102, 118
Gogo 119
grammar 4, 6, 17, 19, 21, 23, 36, 39, 43–6;
  universal grammar 14–15
Greece 31, 96
Greek civilization 4, 31, 82; language 41, 68,
  71, 96, 98, 105
Grimm, Jacob and Wilhelm 72

Haeckel, Ernst 105
Hanafi, Amira 82–3
Haugen, Einar 105
Hebrew 13, 68, 98
Hindi 50, 58–9, 114–15; Hindustani 59;
  Hinglish 116
Hitler 107
Holocaust 34

Honda 72, 73
Hong Kong 43, 54, 84
humanism 28, 106; posthumanism 106
Humboldt, Alexander von 29, 105; Wilhelm
  von 29, 105
Huntington, Samuel 52, 73, 103

identity 4, 5, 6, 18, 25, 32, 45; markers of
  identity 6, 10, 18, 51, 56, 60, 80, 103,
  112; national identity 5, 25, 69, 79; *see
  also* language
ideology 3, 4, 15, 28, 40, 79, 92, 101–2, 108,
  109; *see also* language
IELTS 75
Ifugao 113–14
imagined communities 6, 25, 26, 31–4, 38,
  51, 80
Incas 27
India 50, 58–9, 60, 71, 74, 114–16
Indonesia 44, 59; *Bahasa Indonesia* 59
instinct 14, 23; language-as-instinct 15
intercultural competence 73
Inuit 99
Ireland 30, 53, 94, 98; Irish 31, 98
Islam 28, 43, 53, 56, 87, 101, 103
Israel 53, 98
Italy 6, 46, 57, 73, 96; Italian 6, 20, 33, 46,
  60, 68, 71, 74, 82

Japan 44, 52, 72–3, 116; Japanese 44, 52, 54,
  57–8, 74
Javanese 44
Jewish 19, 95, 98
Johnson, Samuel 7

Kachru, Braj 69, 70
Kenya 50, 73
killer language 88
Kinyarwanda 120–1
Kirundi 120–1
kiss squeaks 22
KLM 73
Kloss, Heinz 38, 39
Kongo language 33
Koran 28
Korean 52, 54
Kosovo 79, 82, 126–7; Battle of 79, 80
Kulturnation 29
Kurds 26, 84, 97; Kurdish 97

L2 50–1, 53, 55, 57–8
Ladino 95
language: artificial vs natural 3, 17, 27;
  beliefs 3, 4, 8–9, 28, 101; construction
  3–9, 19–20, 36, 38, 40–3; correct 4, 11,

14, 30, 46, 103, 108; death 9, 92, 93, 95, 96, 98, 99; diversity 19, 76, 96, 105–6, 107, 112; ecology 9, 28, 29, 95, 101, 105–9; endangered 62, 96, 97, 98; ethnicity 29, 30, 31, 80, 111, 119, 123, 124, 126; heritage 33, 43, 84, 90, 98, 113; histories 8, 9, 111–29; identity 4–6, 10, 18, 20, 25–6, 29, 77, 84, 108; ideologies 3–4, 27–9, 43, 46, 75, 79; indigenous 55, 61, 84, 94, 96, 97, 106, 113, 120, 122, 123; instinct 14–15, 23, 67; loss 18, 77, 90, 95–6; management 8, 9, 102; myth 3, 8, 9, 13, 15, 26, 27, 101; policy 29–30, 39, 42, 55, 56, 64, 72, 88, 89, 109; politics 4, 6, 7–8, 9, 14, 39, 49, 53, 71, 73–4, 79, 86, 101; prestige 7, 36, 43, 55, 56, 57, 61, 63–4, 68, 86, 88, 93–4, 96–7, 98, 103, 104; purification 43, 46, 81, 93; revival 31, 98, 122; standard 26, 37, 60, 103; struggle 7, 17, 30, 79, 83, 85, 86, 88, 97, 107; testing 70, 75; thought 4, 7, 10, 14, 16, 21; threat 7, 10, 29, 56, 79, 84, 88, 90, 96, 99; war 7, 9, 28, 40–1, 46, 79, 83, 85

Latin 6, 7, 37, 39, 61, 68, 69, 77, 94, 96, 98; *see also* alphabet

Latin America 6, 52, 55, 84, 89, 112, 123–6

Leopold I 86

liberal 30, 68,

liberalism 28; neo-liberalism 53, 102

lieu de mémoire 79, 82, 126

Lingala 94

lingua franca: Arabic 56; Chinese 11; Dutch 60; English 11, 18, 32, 53, 70, 71, 87, 104, 107, 109; French 63; German 57; Malay 59; Russian 56; Swahili 120

linguistic determinism 16; ecosystem 99, 105–7; engineering 17, 30; human rights 89; imperialism 89, 106, 124; inertia 68

Lloyd George, David 73–4

Low Countries 39, 60, 86

Macau 54, 58

Macedonia (North) 31, 126

macrolanguage 54, 56, 62

Macron, President 104

Magellan, Ferdinand 97

Malay 50, 52, 59, 60

Mandarin *see* Chinese

Manx 31

Maori 17–18, 123

Mao Zedong 43, 54

Marathi 59

Marx, Karl 7; *das Kapital* 28

May, Stephen 6

metaphor 7, 79, 80, 82, 83, 85, 88, 92, 93, 101

Mexico 55

Milošević, Slobodan 80, 107, 126

mission civilisatrice 55, 60

monolingualism 90

Montenegrin 39, 49; Montenegro 49, 126

More, Thomas 68

mother tongue 94, 101, 114, 119, 121, 127

Mubarak, Hosni 101, 118

multicultural 25, 87, 90, 98, 107, 127

multi-ethnic 123, 124, 126

multilingual 6, 7, 19, 62, 69, 70, 74, 85–6, 90, 95, 105, 119

names of countries 31, 37, 86; of languages 6, 31, 37, 38, 39, 49, 59, 102; of people 40, 42, 72, 97, 122; of streets and cities 40, 41

Napoleon 5, 86

narratives 9, 19, 27, 28, 79, 80, 82, 83, 87, 88, 90, 102, 105, 111, 112

Nasser, Gamal Abdel 56

nation 5–6, 7, 25–7, 28–30, 31, 38, 53, 61, 81; nation-building 26, 27, 30, 48, 72, 84, 88, 103; nation-state 6, 26, 30, 38, 49, 62, 63, 64, 96, 99, 108

national identity 10, 25, 69, 79; language 17, 31, 59, 60, 68, 77, 109, 113, 119, 121

nationalism 10, 27, 28, 29, 37, 42, 63, 80, 87, 89, 90, 98, 116, 126

native language 10, 19, 48, 86, 87, 94, 96, 97, 123; speaker 20, 34, 50, 51, 59, 69, 70, 74, 75, 95, 104, 109, 113, 127

nativism 89

nativization 93

natural selection 93

Nazism 21, 29, 38, 40, 64, 80, 95

Netherlands 8, 37, 39, 41, 60, 61, 64, 70, 76, 86, 87, 95, 97, 127

New Englishes 74, 94

Newspeak 4, 21

Newton 68

New Zealand 17, 53, 94, 98, 99, 112, 122–3

Nicaragua 123–4

Nim Chimpsky 22, 102

Nissan 72

Norman French 67

Norway 30, 45; Norwegian 38, 45, 105, 127

Nović, Sara 18

Occitan 19

Ogden, Charles Kay 20

Orwell, George 4, 21, 28, 42, 109; *Animal Farm* 28; *Nineteen Eighty-Four* 4, 21; *Politics and the English Language* 4
Ottoman Empire 42, 43, 79, 118, 126

Pakistan 58–9, 73, 115
Palenque 32–3, 96
parallel lingualism 109
Pennycook, Alastair 6, 106, 108
personal language histories 8, 9, 111–12
Pessoa, Fernando 7
Philippines 53, 112, 113–14
Phillipson, Robert 89
pidgin 58, 93–4
Pinker, Steven 10, 15, 30, 96
Plattdeutsch 38
pluricentric 39
Poirot, Hercule 71
Polari 32
politics 4, 6–9, 14, 39, 49, 53, 73–4, 79, 87; *see also* language
Portugal 58; Portuguese 6, 7, 50, 53, 58, 94, 103, 116, 123
Power Language Index 51–2
pragmatism 11, 20, 60, 67, 72, 103, 104; Anglo-Saxon Pragmatism 28
Prague Manifesto 19
pronouns 37–8, 43–5
pronunciation 6, 29, 32, 33, 40, 56, 70, 93, 102; received pronunciation 33

Quebec 55
Quechua 62, 102

race 5, 6, 10, 32–3, 50, 70, 106
rationalism 10, 15, 28–9
Real Academia de la Lengua Española 39, 46
religion 4–6, 10, 15, 25, 28, 39, 53, 55, 58, 67, 81, 87, 96, 102–5
Rivarol, Antoine de 10, 29
Romance languages 6, 19, 55, 94
Romanticism 28–9, 88, 96
Russel, Bertrand 102
Russia 7, 55, 56–7, 62, 88; Russian language 56–7, 62, 63, 74, 76, 82, 104, 125, 126
Russian Revolution 44, 88
Russification 56, 88

Sanskrit 61, 98
Sapir-Whorf hypothesis 16, 96
Sarajevo 39, 84–5
Sartre, Jean-Paul 71
Scandinavia 38, 45, 64, 70, 109, 127; Scandinavian English 104

Schwyzerdütsch 38
Scotland 26, 30, 94; *Scotticisms* 46
secularism 92, 103
Serbia 49, 79, 80–2, 126–7; Serbian 39, 49, 82, 126
Serbo-Croatian 39, 81
sex 32, 45–6, 118
Shaw, G.B. 40
Siemens 72
sign language 17–19, 20, 22, 32
Sindhi 114–15
Sissi, Abdel Fattah el 118
Slavic languages 19
Slovene 99; Slovenia 99
Snow White 71–2, 77
Sodexo 72
South Africa 7, 37, 53, 60, 69, 94
Soviet socialism 28
Spain 6, 31, 44, 46, 55, 58, 60, 67, 84, 96, 98, 99, 108; colonization 27, 41, 49, 55, 60, 67, 94, 113; language policy 31, 84, 98
Spanish 6–8, 33, 38–9, 41, 44, 55–6, 61, 74, 76, 97, 103; in Latin America 33, 44, 50, 52, 61–2, 97, 123–4, 124–5; in the United States 68, 89–90
spelling 4, 6, 17, 18, 32, 38–9, 80, 95, 103; wars 40–3
Staatsnation 30
Stalin 104, 126
standard language 10, 18, 26, 30, 36, 39, 46, 63; standardization 16, 27, 37, 38, 48, 77, 93, 94, 102, 103, 105
Streep, Meryl 34
superdiversity 32, 70
survival of the fittest 92–3
Swahili 50, 53, 94, 119, 120–1
Sweden 55, 88; Swedish 7, 38, 45, 88, 89, 127; *Swedishization* of Finland 88
Switzerland 7, 38, 55, 57, 85, 95
Syria 26, 32, 84, 97

Tagalog 113–14
Tahrir Square 82–3
Taiwan 43, 54, 112, 116–17
Tanzania 53, 57, 73, 112, 119–20
Thane 114–15
Thatcher, Margaret 34
Tibet 83
Tito 39
TOEFL 75
tonal language 54
Tordesillas, Treaty of 58
Toubon Law 64
translanguaging 127

translating 41, 44, 48, 58, 64, 68, 71, 72, 75, 77, 80, 90, 97, 104, 118–19, 120; translatability between species 21
tribalization 107
tsunami of English 7, 79, 88, 93
Turkey 26, 32, 43, 56, 61, 84, 97, 103; alphabet revolution 42; language revolution 42–3
Turkish 42–3, 61, 81, 126
Tuwali 113–14

United Kingdom 6, 8, 18, 32, 53–4, 69, 75, 86, 89, 96, 97, 117
United Nations 26, 31, 74, 97, 106
United States 5, 11, 18, 33, 34, 40, 46, 49, 52, 53–4, 56, 61, 64, 67–9, 73, 75, 89–90, 96, 104, 117, 123–5
upward social mobility 86, 98
Urdu 58–9, 115
Utopia 86

vernacular 68, 77, 94, 115, 119

Vietnam 43; Vietnamese 42–3
vocabulary 4, 6, 17, 19, 21, 30, 36, 39, 43–6, 67, 128

Wales 30, 86, 94; Welsh 4, 82
Wallonia 8, 41, 55, 86–7
Waterloo, Battle of 73
Webster, Noah 40; Merriam-Webster 44
Weinreich, Max 36
wild children 16
William the Conqueror 67
Wilson, Woodrow 73
Wittgenstein, Ludwig 7
Woolf, Virginia 7
world language 9, 19, 49, 53, 67–71

Yaghan 97
Yiddish 34, 36, 37
Yugoslavia 31, 39, 49, 53, 80, 82–3, 85, 126–7

Zamenhoff, L.L. 19